Richard,

Only this love,

Lyn Mayo

The Wave

The Wave

Flowing As Essence

Lyn Mayo, Ed.D.

BLUE DOLPHIN

Published by
Blue Dolphin Publishing, Inc.
P.O. Box 8, Nevada City, CA 95959
Orders: 1-800-643-0765
Web: www.bluedolphinpublishing.com

ISBN: 1-57733-151-6

First edition: March, 2005

Library of Congress Cataloging-in-Publication Data

Mayo, Lyn, 1938-
    The wave : flowing as essence / Lyn Mayo.— 1st ed.
        p. cm.
    Includes bibliographical references (p.   ).
    ISBN 1-57733-151-6 (pbk. : alk. paper)
    1. Self. 2. Consciousness. 3. Identity (Psychology) I. Title.

BF697.M39 2005
204'.4—dc22
                                          2005004129

"Go with the Flow" image from OSHO ZEN TAROT by Osho.
Copyright © 1994, Osho
International Foundation, Switzerland. www.osho.com

Author photo: Christopher Briscoe www.chrisbriscoe.com

Lyric excerpts from "This Embrace" © 1999 Kirtana /℗ 1999 Wild
Dove Music / BMI and from "A Deeper Surrender" © 2002 Kirtana /
℗ 2002 Wild Dove Music / BMI
All Rights Reserved.

Printed in the United States of America

5   4   3   2   1

With Appreciation and Gratitude

for

My Many Teachers

Contents

Preface

THERE IS A DEEP URGE WITHIN EACH OF US to know what this existence is all about, to know who we are, to know why we are here. It may be a longing for truth or peace, or a longing to end the suffering and become self-realized. For some, this urge is deeply buried. For others, it resides just below the surface, periodically making itself known. For still others who have committed their lives to discovering truth, this longing is a constant companion. A significant number of people live in devotion to the truth that they know and are ever deepening their capacity to *be* that truth. Wherever we find ourselves in our own evolution is just where we are, and it is absolutely perfect.

This book is focused on the process of unfolding, on discovering the truth of who one is, one's connection to all that is, and the endless discoveries of what it is to be divine consciousness in a human form. Many of us are living our lives devoted to expanding our understanding of Essence, to deepening our capacity to be in our hearts, and to increasing our willingness to surrender. Each of us has our own unique process of dissolving the illusion inherent in this relative reality in which we live and embracing the absolute reality that is the truth of all existence. We experience some commonality in this adventure. My hope is that exploring both our commonality and honoring our individual uniqueness can be useful to each of us.

What is written here is not sacred; nothing said on these pages is to be "believed." Truth lies within our own selves at the core of our own beings. If something written here resonates with your own knowing, honor this with devotion in your heart. Some of the words may not coincide with truth as you know it and need to remain right here on these pages. I encourage you to let yourself be open, but not to allow a blanket acceptance of anything you read here that may seem plausible, yet is not currently your own experience of truth. At best, something that sounds possible may sufficiently expand your constructs to open the door and allow access to you own inner knowing. You may discover it is indeed truth, or you may find it is something you truly don't know. Freedom exists in discovering you just don't know, and that is fine. Furthermore, you may never know, and that is also fine.

To attempt to describe in words that which is indescribable is folly, yet the written word is what we have to work with. The writing of this book was something I knew I was to do. When I began to write, I was not sure if the reason was for my own integration or for others, possibly even both. To be clear about what I know and don't know and to attempt to put that into words has been illuminating. While writing, the illustrations that often came to mind were from my own life. This was very helpful for my own integration. When it became clear that I would share this book with others, I wrestled with including these examples in the book. At one point in the book, I suggest that people give up their stories, and yet here I am including portions of my own spiritual story. Despite that reservation, I have included them here in the hope that they lend some grounding and humanness to what I am attempting to share. As a preamble, this background may be helpful.

Life itself, and many people in this life, have been my teachers. I have found great richness in the exposure to various traditions. I grew up active in the Presbyterian Church, with family members and a husband who were clergy of that denomination. Later, I spent fifteen years in the practice of meditation, often spending time visiting an ashram in upstate New York near where I lived, as well as an ashram in India. Later still, I was fortunate to spend time with Gangaji, an American teacher, and John de Ruiter, a Canadian, both of whom have deeply integrated the East and the West. These experiences have flavored what is written here.

Over the past four years, the music of Kirtana has pierced my heart and validated some of my understandings. Often, I sing one of her beautiful songs to greet the day. Each chapter begins with some of the exquisite poetry that is her songs. With great respect and pleasure, I share some of her lyrics here with you. If they speak to you also, and you wish to have more information, how to reach her can be found under sources at the back of the book.

> May we all deepen our awareness of the wave,
> Trusting the flow to sustain and provide.
> May we each return again and again to the love that *is* us
> Until we become so immersed that we never leave
> The awareness of who we truly are.

The Wave

I'll let this love carry me
Downstream like a petal of prasad
Uproot and ferry me
From the heart of illusion
To the heart of God

from "This Embrace" by Kirtana

The Flow of the Wave

ALL THAT EXISTS IS CONSCIOUSNESS, flowing as a wave, creating
form and moving through form. In this relative reality in which
we live, we are consciousness in the form of a human being.
Consciousness is us and flows through us. Everything we see
is consciousness in form. Nothing exists but this flow of
creation. Essence is infinite, so vast it seems that we will not,
at least while in this form, fully comprehend its magnificence.
The most expanded mind, the most wide-open heart, bows in
reverence to that little bit that is known of the depths of
consciousness.

We can seek to describe our understanding of Essence by
using metaphors familiar to us on this earth plane. In so
doing, we are attempting to describe the indescribable. Given
this severe limitation, perhaps the metaphor of a wave can be
useful. From the perspective of our relative reality, as our
awareness expands, we can experience ourselves as being on
the wave that both flows through and is all of creation. As we
become more aware that we are this wave, we discover it
could not be otherwise; there is no other way to be. The wave
of consciousness is everything. Essence is consciousness. We
have access to the awareness of the wave as it flows through
the core of our innermost being. The silence of our hearts is
where we can most easily experience ourselves flowing with
the wave in the ocean of consciousness, at harmony with all
that is.

While in this human form, we experience the illusion of
separation from Essence. It is just that—an illusion. In absolute reality, all that exists is pure consciousness; there is no
human form, no wave, and no ocean separate from that.
However, since we have taken birth into relative reality as a

seemingly separate form, we are slowly finding our way through the illusion, longing to discover the truth of the oneness of our existence.

We can experience ourselves flowing with the wave of consciousness in varied individual ways. One way is that as we fully awaken to the present moment, we become aware of the process of moving with the wave of consciousness as it flows around and within us, while exposing us to truth through every circumstance in our lives. Being the wave is an ever-deepening process that can unfold into moment-to-moment awareness of who we truly are, as well as open us to peak experiences that reveal the truth of our oneness with Essence. In this way, we move forward through life, flowing with the wave.

There is very little stagnancy, very little holding on, very little wanting to figure out, and much more movement, action, manifestation, and collaboration. We absorb experiences that reveal the union of what is. Not just what is here, but what is everywhere. We have a sense of always moving through depth and substance. Everything perceived from the viewpoint of absolute consciousness reveals a clarity that is experienced as we move through life. We continually deepen our awareness in such a way as to allow the revelation of truth into every moment, and in doing so we simultaneously, very strongly, reaffirm that truth.

This way of being with the wave is a replica of the very foundation of the universe. Unity allows itself to appear in particular forms only to dissolve back into unity. As we expand our awareness, we begin to see everywhere the replication of this pattern of unity, apparently breaking into components to eventually coming back to unity. By taking birth into form, we seemingly separated from Essence and perceive ourselves as separate from other forms that inhabit this earth plane. Eventually we will all come to realize we are all that from which we came.

Another example of this might be that, as we grow and develop, we create with our minds tightly held beliefs or mental constructs. As we become more aware, these constructs start breaking down into components, only to dissolve into the realization that we don't know, into the clarity of truth.

Each of us has the capacity for real connection, real union, with Essence. Actually, we are always in union with Essence. All that is missing is our awareness of that inherent, inseparable state. We celebrate when we realize we are not really flowing on or with a wave and have an experience that we *are* the wave. The continual awareness of oneness with the wave is not automatic after such realizations. The deepening understanding, the expansion of the heart, and the surrender to flowing as Essence continues throughout our lifetimes. Continual noticing and dexterity helps us to remain in awareness of being one with the wave of creation.

Silence of the Heart

ALL THAT EVER HAPPENS in any given moment is that we are aware of the wave or we are not. The wave exists and we are being supported and sustained by it, even when we are not aware of the sustenance. The easiest access to the wave is in simply sensing its flow through the silent core of our being. Such an awareness dramatically changes how we perceive the events in this story we call a life.

Being with the wave does not guarantee an easy, pain-free life. Quite the contrary, the more we remain in moment-to-moment awareness of the wave, the more open, receptive, and vulnerable we become. Whatever life offers up, no matter how difficult the experience, it does not topple one whose foundation of individual being is consciously attuned to the flow of Essence. The heart is pierced, pain may be experienced. However, it moves quickly through the body.

Being the wave means that one is not stagnant. The more we connect with the presence of the wave, the less dramas are able to establish residence in our lives. We may greet a formerly perceived difficult situation as an opportunity to let go of a burden we have been lugging around. The longer we remain in awareness of our roots in the wave, the more we deepen the capacity to experience previously loaded circumstances with surprising detachment. We discover ourselves present in the event, but no longer involved in the drama.

When we choose to tune in, the singing of the heart emanating from the core of our being is a constant companion on the wave. The melody is a joyful love song that can hold and rock each of us, no matter what events are unfolding. Sometimes, the singing is a joyful presence, creating a sense of sunshine to accompany our every moment. At other times, we experience ourselves enveloped in a deep stillness, a solid presence of peace in the depth of our hearts, even as intense feelings inhabit the foreground of our attention.

Some call this sensation in the heart a sense of being home. Others speak of a fire burning inside their chest. Here it is being spoken of as an awareness of the flow of the wave running through our innermost being in the core of the heart. However it is perceived is just perfect. It is the elixir of life, the teacher of gratitude, for it fills the heart with overflowing abundance.

Eventually, we realize we do not know where the wave is taking us, and not knowing doesn't matter. We discover we do not need to be afraid of the unknown or to place what is unfolding into a fixed belief system. What is happening is changing so quickly that we do not need to hold on to or have a certain vantage point about anything. This produces a deep trust, a resting in the knowing that we are being nourished and sustained by the creative force flowing through our being.

What remains constant is the devotion to that little bit of truth that we know. All else can be in flux while we enjoy the flow.

At times in all our lives, we appear to be swimming fast to get to something, searching, hoping to attain a desired goal. At those times, we are no longer one with the flow. We perceive ourselves as the doer in charge of the course and speed of the flow. This perception may be either temporary or deeply implanted, but the wave of creation will flow by itself regardless of our folly. Glorious are those times when we flow effortlessly, relishing a sense of harmony with Essence.

At other times, we move sideways across the current attracted by some diversion, some desire, something we perceive we want or need. We may either have a glimpse or an almost continual awareness that everything we need or could ever want is inside us, ever available as we connect with the flow in the core of our being. Yet, in the moment, we may be attracted to something we see on the horizon and find ourselves madly swimming across the current toward something that is our desire. At these times, the swim takes much more energy and can be stressful if not a downright struggle. Or we attempt a backstroke, struggling against the flow and making our lives abundantly difficult, all the while hoping to return to the familiar, to that which seems safe. Or we might choose to climb out of the water and just rest and hang out on our raft with its umbrella overhead and piña colada in hand.

But eventually, the wave will toss us into the deep where we can either quickly struggle back to our raft, or instead we can choose to explore the bounties of the dark, apparent nothingness of the deep. Whichever is fine, for there will be another toppling of the raft, another opportunity to explore no-thing-ness, and eventually, one discovers such comfort in being in the void that fear subsides. The gifts of the deep are bountiful.

We can judge ourselves for forgetting the wave and creating these obstructions. Married to such judgments can be guilt and shame, which are heavy burdens that make the lightness of flowing as Essence even more difficult. The truth is that the judgments belong to us, not the wave of consciousness. Consciousness doesn't really care. There is no timeline for us to achieve anything. There is no destination for us to arrive at. We are the wave, aware or not, and we are supported, upheld, and nourished by a love the depth and breadth of which is beyond our comprehension or ability to describe. This love and support remains no matter how rough the ocean of life events, and is present whether we are in harmony with or struggling against the flow.

Discovering
the Wave

Your Beloved calls you here today
To ask you for this dance
What will you say?
Are you going to throw the chance away?
And do you hear the music
In your heart?
Maybe you should give your mind a rest
And put its main assumption to the test
Just let go and see who leads the best
Surrender to the music
In your heart.
Maybe you don't need to understand
Maybe these are steps that can't be planned
Funny how your feet know where to land
When you listen to the music
In your heart.

from "Do You Hear the Music" by Kirtana

Knowing

MANY OF US ARE AWARE of a deep longing to know the truth. We want to understand. As we flow with the wave of creation, we naturally absorb truth. That which we take in is translated into a cellular vibration representing creation itself. One metaphor for understanding this is to imagine our form's vibration as a big magnet that attracts us to truth. As we flow with the wave, truth is available to penetrate our beings where it expands our understanding and our vibrations. When that which we are absorbing and our own vibrations are sufficiently in harmony, we are open and receptive. At times, what we have opened ourselves to is such a stretch that it feels like our systems have expanded almost to the breaking point. That which is too discordant does not attract us or we are not receptive. Truth will not disappear; it is always available in the flow, and we can open to it at any time.

Usually when we speak of knowing something, it is a concept we understand with our minds. Here we are speaking of a knowing that comes from deep within the heart. This knowing can take several forms. In the first way of knowing, truth exists as a cellular imprint that has not been conceptualized by the mind and doesn't initially come into words that can be grasped by a mental process. Much of this is energetically absorbed and our understanding is non-verbal. One example of this could be the transmission of energy from a spiritual teacher. Another is the absorption of energy in a sacred space, where one finds oneself quieter inside. This might be a temporary quieting, or with sufficient exposure, a change in one's vibration. The following is an example from my life:

In 1980, I decided I wanted to learn to meditate in hopes of slowing down my life. So I attended an introductory session at a nearby ashram designed for people interested in exploring meditation. While there, I was introduced to Swami Muktananda, the head of the ashram. I vividly remember the moment I met his eyes, and my whole world spun. I returned to my seat stunned, trying to make some sense out of what had just happened. It was my first conscious experience of the transmission of energy. I recall thinking that this must be a mild version of the energy people spoke about experiencing around Jesus.

Two things Muktananda said that day rang true, but I did not have a clue as to what they meant. The first was that everything I needed to know was inside me. The second was that God dwelled in me as me. Two very simple statements, yet I spent the next twenty years moving through many layers of depth in order to understand their truth.

In a second manner of knowing, truth is absorbed and resonates in our innermost being in such a way that we just know its validity. We might hear something that rings of truth, and we know deep within us it is just that: truth. A realization may bubble up from inside, and we know our innermost is surfacing with truth. That knowing does not come from the mind; it is a knowing of the heart.

The following event happened in my life after being involved with meditation for twelve years and is an ordinary example of what I mean by this form of knowing.

While attending a workshop on contemplation at the same ashram, I was startled to hear my name called. I was asked to stand along with seven others as we towered over the some two thousand meditators seated cross-legged around us on the floor of the ashram's main hall. A swami from the staff of Gurumayi Chidvalasanda, Muktananda's successor, proceeded to ask those of us standing a question related to her morning talk. He first addressed a woman in the front, far to my right, and then began working his way across the room as he expanded upon what had been said. I attempted to listen, but as he moved closer, anxiety took over my brain. *What will he ask me? What if I don't know the answer? I hate this! Why me? He doesn't even know my name. I have never been put on the spot before. Why now?*

I closed my eyes, deepened my breathing, and concentrated on sensing my feet on the floor, my legs underneath me. Slowly, I could feel my body relax and the chatter subside. When I opened my eyes, he was looking right at me, his face betraying no feelings, giving no clues. The question, when it finally came, was not about the morning program, but instead a question I had rarely heard asked: "Who are you?" Without thought, from deep inside me, the response rolled forth: "I am perfection."

At first, my answer startled me, but as I quieted inside, I knew the truth of it. Swami did not move. "Who are you, really?" he asked again. "I am absolutely perfect," I responded unflinchingly. The truth of it deepened, embedding itself in an internal quiet. "You have a job; you have a name; you have a family?" he continued. I looked away. It occurred to me that he actually wanted to know my name. However, I just nodded. When I returned to look at him I said, "Perfection is who I am. I am not the rest."

Swami stood gazing at me for what seemed an eternity. Suddenly he smiled, nodded, blessed me with a loving look, and then quickly moved on to the next person, the next question. A love from deep inside filled my chest, and I no longer listened. I was immersed in peace. What peace! I had my first small glimpse of that peace that is beyond understanding.

Finally, we discover truth through direct experience. This could take the form of a dramatic realization such as an experience of recognizing who we truly are or a merging with Essence.

Gangaji often uses a form of self-inquiry with people who bring her their concerns by suggesting they get in touch with what they are feeling in that moment. She then suggests that they let themselves become immersed in the feeling until it totally consumes them. Usually, another feeling emerges that was underneath the first, so she suggests that they now be with this new feeling, to see what is even deeper. Frequently, people continue this process until they discover ... "nothing."

The first time I was in a silent retreat with Gangaji was in Lake Tahoe, the summer of 1999. I was sitting with the group, feeling a lot of pain in my heart regarding a relationship with a man who had decided to be with a much younger woman. They were sitting across the room from me.

Gangaji was up front talking to a person who was dismayed regarding his recurring involvement with alcohol. I remember thinking that I was there at the retreat for a purpose, and I could either wallow in my suffering or silently become involved in the same process Gangaji was taking this man through. I let myself feel the surface pain, then the pain of not being enough, and then my loneliness. This continued until I was surprised to find myself in a vast void. I had experienced this void before, so it was familiar. This time, however, my physical boundaries vanished, and there was no me, no body, no mind, just intelligent awareness. I discovered that this void was not just nothing. It was alive, silent, pure consciousness, and I was that.

Gangaji had been right when she said, "In the core of everything is the most unbelievable, unimaginable revelation." Kirtana speaks of the divine appearance in the following verse from one of her songs: "You appear in the heart of fear and each drop of pain, like a gem buried underground. Who would think of looking here for signs of your grace? Ah, but there is no place where you cannot be found."

The knowing coming from such experiences radically transforms our perception of truth. Such a change in our understanding may take some time for us to integrate into our life experience.

Less dramatic but equally important to our unfolding are the day-to-day experiences of surrender, the moment-to-moment *being* the truth that we know. These ordinary experiences open us to enable truth to reveal itself, as well as help us integrate new understanding. When we realize that we have let go of false identity, we know our perception of reality has changed. What has also changed is our cellular vibration. We have become cleaner and clearer.

The Search for Understanding

FOR MOST OF US, when we first started on our spiritual quests, we had the misguided hope that if we could just understand the mysteries with our minds, that understanding would take us home. Thus, the search for understanding began.

We did not yet realize that expanding our awareness through a knowing of the heart was the essential key. Such awareness is radically different from any previous undertaking in which we tried to understand something with our minds or our intuition. We have been schooled to undertake a course of study in order to obtain some desired learning. However, it soon becomes apparent that in order to discover the truth that we seek, a course in comparative religion will not suffice.

On a much more subtle level, a study course is what many of us undertake by creating our own individual curriculum. Friends recommend books that have been meaningful to them, so we pick them up to read. Sometimes, our hearts may be touched deeply by something we read or hear that awakens our own awareness. Gradually, the books we are attracted to change, and we find ourselves drawn to books written by those who have had great depth of understanding. We hear of a workshop on a new kind of meditation, so we sign up and partake. Some of us travel halfway around the world to India or Tibet to be with a particular teacher or bask in the energy of a known sacred site. None of this is in error, for it may facilitate a sufficient shaking of the foundation of our tightly held mental concepts and thus begin to make room for a deeper knowing in the heart.

For those of us who have been steeped in a particular religion with its tenets and cultural traditions, this expansion may at first be disturbing. Securely held constructs may begin to break down, leaving us unsettled as we no longer have assurance in the validity of what we thought we knew. Even though this shake-up may be disorienting, our willingness to tolerate not knowing is an essential ingredient to our liberation. In not knowing, we leave room to experience truth. We realize we have been there before, been shaken-up and survived. If you remember your childhood concept of God, your more mature current understanding is probably considerably different.

If it is truth we say we want, then we must surrender the idea that it will take the form we wish it to take. We may have a good giggle at ourselves when it begins to dawn that we have been on a search for truth while already having a confirmed idea of the form in which it should appear. Such a search is obviously madness. Seeking truth is futile when such a quest is really a cover for wanting an affirmation of what we already believe and hold sacred. Truth will not alter itself to fit our desires. We can continue to hold our beliefs sacred and create a filter through which truth may or may not be able to penetrate. The cellular vibration created by our possibly rigid commitment to these beliefs may make it difficult for us to attract and open to deeper truths. Or, we can trust enough to enter the space of not knowing and be available to truth.

One metaphor we can use to describe a "spiritual journey" is a wheel with many spokes all leading to the same hub. Some teachers advise seekers to travel one spoke to the hub. A spoke is a particular tradition or set of practices. The recommendation to remain on one spoke has several purposes beyond the hope that a straight line may be the shortest way between where you are and where you wish to be, assuming one does not get stuck along the way. One purpose is to establish a particular practice, such as a form of meditation that can be steadfastly ridden to the core rather than jumping from spoke to spoke when the going gets tough. One of the difficulties with the metaphor of a "spiritual journey" is that it is linear, implying an end path often called "enlighten-ment" or "going home." When we get there, we have suppos-edly "arrived." The truth is that our understanding is forever deepening.

If we are bravely honest with ourselves, we will know when fear is causing us to bolt. We will know when we have been distracted and are swimming against the current or madly trying to backstroke. We will also know intuitively when we are being led to a deeper unfolding of truth. True understanding comes from a knowing that is experienced deep within. Clarity comes from being with the wave, both flowing on the surface and allowing ourselves to dive and explore the deeper un-known. Eventually, we realize our oneness with the wave. When we listen to our innermost, we flow as Essence. No prescription exists for being with the truth of your own being. We are each with the wave in our own organic way. Each of us has our own guidance.

We may attempt to put this clarity into words, but words often fail us. They are an attempt to confine that which has no boundaries. We think we know what a particular word means, yet again and again, we discover another layer of meaning. Personally, I experienced times when reading or listening to a new teacher, who phrased something differently, facilitated this opening to a new depth. Ultimately, however, the clarity comes from within.

As the spokes of the wheel come to the middle, they get closer together. The same is true as we deepen our under-standing through a particular tradition. As we approach the truth at the core of any tradition, we are able to hear and to understand the commonality in all traditions. Truth is truth. What becomes apparent is that the great sages and saints of various traditions are pointing to the same thing. My experi-ence is that some teachers, both deceased and currently on the planet, speak from the center of the wheel where there is no longer a religion or a tradition, just truth. When we find ourselves in the center of the wheel, we no longer identify ourselves with any tradition, and yet we may find we have respect for all.

As one opens up the cages of previously held concepts and limited understanding, this oneness at the core of all traditions becomes even more apparent. What may have become a rote memorization from one's childhood religious education takes on new depth of meaning as it is heard anew dressed in the garments of a different tradition.

The words of Psalm 46:10, "Be still and know," are heard in a deeper way while reading a similar suggestion made by the beloved Indian sage of the twentieth century, Sri Ramana Maharshi. Eventually, we discover for ourselves that stillness brings us to the silent core of our heart. It is a gateway to the infinite. The sages of many eras have always been pointing us in the direction of a deeper knowing. That direction is inward.

Those of us who have grown up in a Judaic-Christian culture have looked outside ourselves for many of the answers to our deepest questions. Eastern traditions are steeped in practices focused on going within. Most Westerners experience devotion within while involving themselves in spiritual practices relating to a source found solely outside themselves. Throughout society, there is an increased merging of East and West, but particularly in the area of spirituality. In the community in which I live, meditation and contemplation groups now meet regularly in local churches. These groups are not replacing Christian Bible study and prayer groups, but augmenting them.

When we begin to look for answers within, a more dramatic shift takes place than may be initially apparent. For me this transition was to be more complex than I had first realized.

After meeting Swami Muktananda, I gradually became a disciplined meditator, getting up early each morning to meditate and often attending retreats at his nearby ashram. The Siddha Yoga practiced there has its roots in Hinduism. This tradition makes a distinction between the small self, also referred to as the personality, and the larger Self, the divine within. Previous to learning to meditate, my locus for God was outside myself; I prayed to a God in the heavens. Even though at the beginning of my learning to meditate many statements were made that I could find the divine by going within, they did not really penetrate. My access to God had been through prayers I sent out into the universe.

My motivation for meditating was the desire to quiet down a stressful life. I was not seeking truth or self-realization. Focusing and reminding myself that I could have access to God by going within were important. The process did not happen immediately. The folklore among members of the ashram was that Baba Muktananda had said that if someone was a follower of his, they were in one of their last seven lifetimes. I was sure it would take me at least seven, so I had no expectation of becoming self-realized. Self-realization did not seem to me something that could be sought for anyway.

Initially, my concept of the Self was that it was my soul. As meditation deepened, I began to see a blue light while meditating that was accompanied by a feeling of love in my heart. I began to associate being in the company of the inner Self with the emergence of the blue light and the presence of warmth in my chest. Occasionally, I would close my eyes and see bright lights accompanied by a sense of being in a radiant place. I was so startled that my fear response caused the light to disappear. I attributed this reaction to an exaggerated startle reflex coming from my life story, and that I just was not ready to be in this radiant place for any extended visit.

At that time, my concept of the Self was that it was an aspect of the divine that had residence in my heart, but the rest of me was not God. Gradually, my concept of the Self deepened and broadened until I knew that nothing existed that was not Essence. More recently, comfort has replaced fear, and I remain in that radiant place longer.

The answers to our deepest questions can be found within. I cannot emphasize enough the importance of each of us discovering our way of going within, as well as becoming increasingly vigilant regarding our tendency to look outside ourselves for the answers. Others cannot give us the truth we seek. They may be able to point us in the direction of truth, but ultimately truth can only be found within.

Eventually, the imaginary boundaries between inside and outside evaporate. Then one can be aware of one's own presence as the wave, no matter what the activity. The silence within can be experienced whether washing windows or sitting in solitude immersed in the beauty of the sun fading in the west. Our lives become an ever-deepening expression of devotion to that little bit of truth that we know in our hearts. Some would say that their entire life becomes a meditation.

Practices in Search of Understanding

MANY PEOPLE ON A SPIRITUAL QUEST become involved in the practice of meditation. This practice can be very helpful, particularly for those having difficulty turning inward. Most meditators will tell you that their minds become more focused and one-pointed. Others state that their minds are less active, and as the mind becomes quieter, they become more deeply acquainted with the silence within. The instruction commonly given to meditators is to repeat a mantra as a short spiritual reminder. When the mind starts racing off, repeating the mantra will bring the mind back into focus. In a similar way, many find chanting to be a calming, joyful act of devotion that can greatly expand the heart. Chants are often the repetition of God's name.

However, for some people, meditation and chanting may begin to feel like a deterrent. Even repeating mantras and singing chants requires a certain activity of mind. As practices deepen, one more readily encounters the stillness within. As one becomes more aware of this stillness, the deep silence is enticing. Some experience mantra repetition or chanting as keeping them on the surface connected to their minds. Responding to the invitation of silence, one may leave mantras and chants behind.

I do not regret having spent fifteen years in daily meditation practice. I cannot possibly know what my unfolding would have been like if I had not. However, after a time, sitting in silence was what seemed most organic. My purpose here is not to undermine the legitimacy of practices, but to support those who discover that, through its own organic timing, their inner guidance may lead them to discard, temporarily or permanently, what has formerly been useful.

Another example of changes that may appear is a discomfort with liturgy or ceremonies that we once found harmonious. Liturgy evolved as a means for expressing devotion. While we can be respectful of what has meaning for others, we may discover a shift in the way we personally want to express our devotion.

> I recall being at a ceremony in honor of the Goddess. It was not the first such ceremony I attended, but it was the first time I became uneasy. The leader of the ceremony suggested we raise our arms to the heavens, indicating the heavens as the abode of the Goddess. For me, the abode of the Goddess is within; we *are* the Goddess. What I was being asked to do was discordant with what I had come to understand and a hindrance to my expressing devotion and gratitude. I could be present and honor this as a ceremony that was meaningful for others, but it no longer felt organically true for me.
>
> Likewise, at one time, I gathered pictures of teachers and sages and placed them on an altar in my room. Eventually, I took all pictures of teachers off my altar and put a mirror in their

place. Looking at myself in the mirror was a graphic reminder that everything was inside my own being. The sage and the teacher are also within. For a while, the mirror was a wonderful reminder. When I felt more firmly rooted with the wave, the mirror came down as well.

We need to give ourselves permission to express our devotion in ways that feel in harmony with our understanding and appreciation of oneness. Our creativity and inner wisdom will guide us. Again, in sharing changes that took place for me, I do not wish to create a linear scale on which to compare means of expressing devotion, only to suggest that each of us can listen within and celebrate in ways that feel true to us at the time.

Courting the Silence

WE CAN ALSO FACILITATE going within by placing ourselves in situations where we can be in silence for an extended period. A friend of mine went to the outer reaches of Alaska to live by himself. He spoke to no one for an entire year and attributes this sojourn to a deepening connection with his inner silence.

Most of us, especially those actively involved in parenting, can't do something this dramatic, but we can instead find other ways to create the time and space to be in silence. Some may seek out silent retreats organized by a spiritual group. The group energy moving toward a deeper stillness is helpful for them. Others may create their own personal retreat, such as being alone in nature. What is important is to get away from responsibilities, phones, television, and books and to allow oneself just to *be*, resting in awareness of Essence for increasingly longer periods of time.

At first, the aloneness may seem unnerving, but, gradually, we begin to notice all the usual ways of distracting ourselves. We want to read or talk to someone or go to a movie. The mind is so accustomed to activity and its usual ways of being entertained. At first, just being in the moment seems like a stretch. But when we go beyond the impulse of the distraction, we begin to discover moments of peace when the clatter of the mind has diminished. Gradually, we discover what each moment has to offer, most of which we had missed before. Eventually, there come moments of pure awareness where there are no thoughts.

Currently, some sages say that the traditional process of many years of prayer or meditation is no longer essential for our unfolding. At the same time, some teachers from Eastern spiritual traditions still strongly believe that the "secret truths" should not be disclosed, but that students should instead discover the "truths" through involving themselves in many years of practice.

Clearly, we are fortunate to live in a time when change is happening quickly for many people as they discover the truth of their being and when powerful energies on the planet support our unfolding. I feel blessed that so many writers and teachers not only share truth as they know it, but are also willing to point us in the direction of discovering truth for ourselves. Their openness has enabled many, many people now living to know their true identity as Essence.

Not Knowing

ALL ONE NEEDS TO DO is be around some New Age communities to see how easily many have discarded the words and concepts of their early religious traditions only to replace them with new lingo, new concepts. We find much comfort in thinking that we know and that our beliefs are real. We discard limiting concepts, yet in order to maintain that comfort, our tendency is to easily adopt new concepts as truth without actually knowing their validity.

We can hypnotize ourselves with the New Age lingo. We can align ourselves with constructs from a new spiritual culture with which we have become identified, thus creating yet another religion. Or we can open ourselves to the willingness to not know. If we have the courage to be in the limbo of not knowing, we give truth a chance. If we are willing to entertain any possibility and not just accept truth from outside ourselves, we then remove internal blocks created by our preconceptions. We leave ourselves open to be attracted to truth as it appears. Real truth flows as the wave of consciousness and can be accessed in the deepest recesses of our hearts.

The process of letting go of preconceptions of truth is not easy. We may still hang on to accumulated beliefs and concepts, consciously or unconsciously. Doing so feels safe and secure. Shaking up our security can be painful. If we are convinced that truth will take a certain form, we are prone to miss it when it appears in a different form. Yet, if we are willing to risk the discomfort of honestly exploring our beliefs, the process can be illuminating. If we want to live in truth, to liberate ourselves from illusion, we must choose to examine our attachment to every concept or belief. What we often discover are many "sacred cows," beliefs that have simply made us feel good.

Upon gentle scrutiny, it becomes apparent that some beliefs we have are perhaps true, yet we are not sure. Those can go in the "perhaps" category. For example, we may have accumulated some beliefs regarding what life is like after death. These beliefs have been quite reassuring when loved ones have died or even in contemplating our own deaths. But can we be comfortable with not knowing? Can we trust the wisdom of the flow? Will not trusting make any difference in the course of the flow anyway? Essence will flow in truth regardless of whether or not we trust. We can create stories that feel good, that are reassuring, or we can discover how much better it is simply to rest deeply in trusting the flow!

Some religious tenets, beliefs, and concepts are truly just a part of our acculturation and fail to pass our closer scrutiny. Those that no longer ring true can be discarded. Friends may have had varied experiences and know some different aspects of Essence. That is their truth. We may or may not have a similar experience. We can only live truth as we know it in the present moment and rid ourselves of the distortions as they become apparent. As we live in devotion to this truth, our own vibration is altered and a deeper clarity is revealed.

After taking the sword of honesty to our concepts and beliefs, what remains is that little bit of the truth that we know. That little bit of truth is really all we need. A line in one of Kirtana's songs illustrates this: "I cannot see how I missed this before. Who we are is always here, of this I am sure." For each of us, we may feel we really know a few things for sure— not that we think or believe are true, but that we know are true. When we can be still and allow truth to emerge, this knowing emanates from the silent core of our hearts. What-ever glimpse of truth we have is enough. Our devotion to that little bit is all we need to fill our deepest longing. We each can have the experience of knowing who we are and our connec-tion with Essence.

This knowing is not a cognitive knowing of the mind but an awareness that emerges from the depth of one's being. It may come after an experience of the vastness of the nothingness or upon really seeing a sunset. That moment of truth is a confirmation of what is known in the core of one's being. It is not a blanket acceptance of what another has said or written. True knowing comes from one's presence with the wave, one's connection with the flow of creation. Each of us has our own direct access to the truth. We need not accept anyone else's.

Even though I had heard the words, "nothing exists except consciousness," they remained only a concept that *seemed* like truth. Several years later, while in retreats with Gangaji and eventually John de Ruiter, I experienced merging with the infinite and understood that nothing exists, including this form called Lyn that is not Essence.

I can't possibly underscore enough the importance of going within and connecting with the wave. Our minds are habit-ridden. If our God has been only external, it will take some gentle reminders to support the inward connection with the wave.

Be with the wave of this life we find ourselves in, and we will find and come to know ourselves as Essence. The wave of our relative existence flows in the ocean of Essence. Clarity exists in infinite Essence. When aware of our presence with the wave, we can experience that clarity.

Seeing clearly, knowing clarity, emerges when we no longer need to hold on to or have a certain vantage point about anything. When we live our lives in devotion to that little bit of truth we know, we can live our lives with integrity. We experience ourselves as cleaner and clearer, no longer cluttered with that which we hope is so. There is an assurance that what little we have glimpsed of truth is enough.

In the process of searching for the answers to our deepest questions, we gradually discover and are at peace with how little we know. Our tolerance for not having the answers increases. We become less willing to accept the stories we have heard as answers to important questions.

Blessed is the moment when we realize that we understand almost nothing. Simultaneously, we begin to realize that the mysteries do not need to be totally understood, nor can they be. Eventually, it really sinks in that we don't need to understand everything, nor will we ever be able to. If we had an unconscious expectation that getting an "A" in the "spiritual seekers" course would lead to self-realization, we now see the folly of that expectation. With this realization comes great freedom. We can put down the burden of needing to know with our minds. We are willing to open ourselves to all possibilities, letting go of limiting constructs in order to be open to truth. Eventually, all of us will realize ourselves to be one with the unknowable.

Stopping the Search

WE HAVE TAKEN FORM in a world of apparent separateness, a world of duality. Yet strong is the longing of the heart to live in truth, to not feel separate, and to live as one with Essence. What we are searching for is the awareness of absolute reality while living in relative reality. As one becomes more aware of absolute reality, this "abiding in two worlds" can feel a bit schizophrenic. The futility of trying to integrate these two worlds by using mental concepts becomes readily apparent. Clear, also, is that striving and seeking will not provide deeper understanding of absolute reality.

At some juncture, what becomes apparent is that we must stop the search. There is nothing to search for, no place to journey, nothing to do. One needs only to rest and abide in the innermost reaches of the heart, the core of one's being. This realization is met with either relief or despair. It is a moment of surrender.

Perhaps some of us needed initially to be involved in the search. Fortunate are we when we truly stop doing and rest in the stillness of who we are. The great paradox is that we get what we want when the striving stops. No longer searching for

answers, we know we can trust the flow of our natural unfolding. No longer trying to stop the mind, we instead relish the
moments, perhaps even seconds, of stillness. We become
observers of the mind's activity, living in devotion to that little
bit of truth that we know, all the while increasingly abiding in
the heart with the mind as our servant. As we love ourselves
more fully, we open our hearts to the flow of eternal truth.
What we have been looking for is readily available within our
own beings in the stillness of our own hearts.

Knowing the Knower

WHEN WE SURRENDER THE SEARCH for knowledge and discover our
pathway within, we are open to know the knower. We begin to
trust the knower, that which observes, is aware, and abides in
the silence of the heart.

We can befriend the silent knower deep inside who is
eternally aware and unchanging. Who is it that sees? Who is
aware? Who knows? It is us. As we become more familiar with
the knower, trust deepens.

For moments, even mini-seconds, the mind stops, and
awareness is still present, simply observing, with no personal
reference point. We are not thinking about what we are seeing.

Meditators may first become aware their mind has
stopped while in deep meditation—repetition of the mantra
has stopped, so has the chatter of the mind. Others may
make the same discovery as they become still while watching
a fire or an exquisite sunset—just observing in the moment,
not labeling anything, taking in the experience without
thoughts.

Eventually, we discover we can go for long periods with no
mind activity. One can even drive a car down the highway,
present in the moment, keenly aware of what is happening,

but never have a thought. This may sound dangerous, but one is actually a safer driver than an individual who is lost in reliving a past drama or anxious about a fantasy he or she is creating regarding future events. One is present in the moment with no thoughts; the eternal knower is observing and aware. The knower resides in silence, and we have access to this residence as frequently as we want. All we need is the awareness of ourselves as Essence.

As we recognize and identify with the knower, we begin to see the events of our lives through our divine eyes. Such vision provides a detachment from self-absorption. From this vantage, we are immersed in the internal quiet and don't find ourselves enticed or triggered by the usual stimulants. Resting in our internal peace, the dramas that formally seduced us into full participation become apparent. We now realize that the storyteller who creates the dramas abides in the mind.

However we have seen others or ourselves through the filter of our minds has no reality in the presence of *now*. Our thoughts have only to do with past or future, either commenting on past events or projecting into the future. Our mind controls the film of this movie we call our life. As the film is rewound, we relive former events, elaborating on details, rewriting events, and hypnotizing ourselves into a trance regarding others' motives and our own. Or when the film is fast-forwarded, we contemplate future events, anxiously involved in the play of "what if?"

When the mind starts to run off creating dramas, it can be reigned in. Through conscious, impersonal noticing, we become increasingly able to let the mind rest without distractions. In so doing, the mind becomes our servant. We no longer believe our thoughts to be reality. When we live in our minds, thoughts reign supreme. A busy mind can create such a loud clatter that it inhibits our ability to hear the guidance from our innermost truth. Yet, to think of the mind as the enemy would be unfortunate. These minds are exquisite instruments that have been provided for this relative reality. The more we are able to reside in the heart and use the mind as a tool, the more we discover how exhausting getting caught up in the mind is. Freeing ourselves and returning to the stillness is such relief! Gradually, as we increasingly trust the knowing of the heart, the heart and mind become one. We become accustomed to being still and knowing.

We want to live in honesty and truth. Truth is found in the heart. Moment to moment honesty has dissolved the mind's hold as the captain of our lives. Anchored in awareness of the wave, we can simply notice our thoughts and not get lost in thinking, not get captured by the mind. Our minds become quieted. There is less clatter to overpower our awareness of the peaceful, steadfast silence within. We can "be with" a feeling, let the feeling engulf us and have its moment, without allowing the mind to take us on a journey to the land of familiar dramas and suffering.

As we are more frequently aware of our connection with the wave of creation, our readiness to merge with Essence unfolds. Merging is an experience of losing a sense of one's physical boundaries, body, personality, and mind in the realization of oneness with all creation. What remains is an intelligent awareness that experiences the merging. When we realize our oneness with Essence, we discover that there is no internal or external, no "me" or "other," just all that is. That intelligent awareness is the knower, is us, is Essence.

Using Teachers for Our Unfolding

TEACHERS CAN PLAY AN IMPORTANT ROLE in our unfolding by pointing us in the direction of truth. We do not need to reinvent the wheel. Many have come before us and discovered

truth. Some have known that they were to share their understanding. The willingness of these sages to live their lives
committed to their own evolution, and to share their knowledge, humbles me in gratitude. I feel abundantly blessed that
various teachers have come into my life, and I cannot imagine
my own unfolding without their guiding me in the direction of
truth. Some people sense the need to dedicate themselves to
one teacher throughout their evolution. Others find benefit
spending time with several teachers. Some read spiritual
books, some spend time in various spiritual practices, and
some never seek out a spiritual community or a teacher. Each
of us has our own guidance and our own organic way of
unfolding.

I have spoken to many serious seekers who have no wish
to involve themselves with a teacher. Some are avid readers of
spiritual books. I once asked a person fond of reading books
by a particular spiritual teacher what the difference was
between reading about these sessions and being in the room.
My friend's response was that he never thought of the author
as his teacher.

This friend is struggling with surrender, as were several
others I spoke to who were adamant about not wanting a
teacher. Either the very personality trait that makes them so
resolute is what makes surrender more difficult, or they are
listening to their guidance from within. As we are more constantly attuned to our oneness with the wave, we know when
fear is the creator of our stance and when we are going with
the flow.

These disenchanted folks see the behavior of some
followers of teachers and gurus as the greatest deterrent. They
perceive the behavior of those followers as parallel to early
adolescents fawning after rock stars.

This demonstration of adoration comes from a lack of
understanding that what one sees in any teacher is only a

reflection of one's own Self. To place a teacher on a pedestal is to put one's Self one down. In addition, anyone we place on a pedestal is bound to fall off. One can perceive a teacher as a master and still hold the awareness that nothing exists within that person that is not present within oneself. We inhabit the space we perceive even the most evolved teacher inhabiting. The difference is that the teacher may be aware of their habitat, and we have yet to discover it. Who we are is already one with Essence. Using our minds to construct a concept of a teacher so far down a linear path, in a place beyond our possibility of venturing, is to construct a mental block to our own awakening.

Some people see in their teacher an idealized parent, lover, or friend. In the field of psychology, this process is called transference. We can transfer onto other people positive and negative aspects of ourselves. We can also place on them assumptions regarding their feelings and behaviors. These assumptions are repeats of those we experienced with important people in our earlier lives and which we now replay to create fresh emotional reactions. What others may be mirroring are beliefs about ourselves that we have internalized.

Our personalities' projections onto a therapist or a spiritual teacher are all gold for our understanding. The gold is in seeing them as a mirror that reflects ourselves. That which we idealize in another is an aspect of ourselves. That which we assume another feels about us, and which creates an emotional reaction within us, is usually something we believe about ourselves. If we catch ourselves denying what we see in the mirror, we may wish to ask ourselves, "Who is it that perceives differently?" It is our mind. Our mind's perception of who we are is not truth.

On a personality level, we can become very attached to another form and not realize that our love for a teacher's form is only a precursor to the unbounded love for the formless.

Such love may play an important role in the expansion of our hearts. However, we can be so enchanted by the form of our beloved guide that we remain in duality, forgetting that we are one with our teacher.

Of the teachers I have seen, Gangaji is a joy to watch as she consistently acknowledges people's feelings regarding the form called Gangaji while at the same time gently turning them back around to themselves. She reminds them that she is only a mirror, a reflection of who they truly are. She repeatedly states that she is not a saint, but rather an ordinary woman, experiencing herself as increasingly more ordinary. She asserts that if she could discover the truth of her being, we can also. I find her stance abundantly refreshing. Even with Gangaji's continual reminders, however, some, for the moment, are unable to hear her. This idealization is a part of their unfolding.

For others, the love they have for their teacher evolves into a mixture of deep gratitude as well and an ever-deepening purity of love. This love for a teacher can develop into a bond that moves beyond idealization. I have not had this close experience with a teacher; so it is not something I can speak to from direct experience. When I have seen such a relationship, I have observed an expansive heart and deep surrender. It seems that such a bond is what the soul organically presents for some. The Self uses whatever it uses to awaken to itself. For those involved in this deep intimacy and openness, what organically evolves is a deep bond. Some have described a sense of their beloved teacher as a living presence within.

Kirtana's willingness to speak of her relationship with her teacher has been a gift for our understanding. All one needs to do is read her words or hear her sing to know that she has a heart that is infinite. Apparently, the cracking open of her heart has in part come from her bond with Gangaji. She speaks of such a bond as the great humbler, constantly cutting through identifications, exposing projections, ruining plans, and piercing hearts with the truth of what is unaffected by change.

Her experience with her teacher has enabled her to write such songs as "My Beloved's Love." A verse from that song so exquisitely states this kind of bond: "And she will crush your sand-like castles, then find you where you hid, and offer you her hand like nothing ever happened, and nothing ever did." Such a relationship may or may not surface in our unfolding, but we can honor it when we see it as an essential ingredient present in the unfolding of another.

Liberation means freedom, and this can sometimes result in behavior that does not fit the norms of the general public. Some evolved beings have been termed eccentric. Others live such quiet lives they go unnoticed in their communities.

Certain teachers and clergy have also exploited followers through personality behaviors that have not yet been cleansed or cleared. I have seen spiritual communities openly confront a teacher, who was behaving in a way they felt suspect, and teachers who have welcomed such encounters. Such openness is refreshing. I have seen other spiritual communities involved in cover-ups, putting a spin on the reports of the teacher's behavior that would win the admiration of the most skilled political spin-doctors. Communities are, after all, made up of human beings with all their frailties. Again, we can use our own discernment, not by using mental concepts or moral judgments, but by listening deep within to our own guidance.

Teachers who facilitate our unfolding give us a gift for which we have no sufficient words of gratitude. Teachers have given me love, respect, guidance, and inspiration throughout my unfolding. There have been those whose beings expressed a truth and integrity that have left me in awe. Some embodied a stillness so profound that just being in their presence enabled me to experience a deeper silence within myself. Others eventually fell off the high pedestal on which I had placed them. Still others, although not fully home themselves, have guided me with respect and as much understanding as they had available. I stand in deep gratitude at the magnitude of each of their gifts.

Life is the paramount teacher. It is far too limiting to confine our teachers to the sages of past or present. Teachers come in many forms—family members and friends, people we meet on the street, nature and life's abundant situations. Whatever we encounter while flowing with the wave is there to teach us.

Even when we work against the flow, the opportunity exists to discover truth. Any happening that enables us to see the illusion more clearly contributes to our unfolding. Perhaps we swim against the flow because we need to experience a situation one more time to see it clearly. When we open our hearts more fully, we allow every situation to teach us. Perhaps we pause for a moment when what we are about to do doesn't feel quite right, trusting our uneasiness and listening within before we proceed. Such a moment is an opportunity to become cleaner and clearer, thus altering our own vibration.

Ultimately, each of us comes to a space where we have sufficiently cleared access to communion within and may not feel we need or want an external teacher. However, discovery of truth never ends, nor does honest noticing. As we open to our inherent capacity to *be* an expression of truth, our unfolding continues. We may place ourselves in the presence of a beloved teacher or not, but we know that truth lies within. Being with the inner knowing is a way of life. There are many realized people on the planet. These are not only teachers but also members of ashrams, monasteries, convents, or members of communities living ordinary lives. Instead of seeing themselves as extra-ordinary, they see themselves as quite ordinary. Indeed they are! Gangaji gives us a great gift in sharing herself as an ordinary woman becoming more ordinary. Apparently, realization is an experience accessible to everyone. How ordinary!

As we are increasingly able to find our direction emanating from the core of our being, we are more readily aware of our choice to listen and be receptive rather than let fear direct our lives. All that is necessary is to allow ourselves to be aware of the wave, and truth makes itself known. Everything we need to awaken to our true nature will appear and reappear until we gradually come out of our sleep and see the dream. Each aspect of our unfolding is important, and no one phase is more important than the next.

We may find it difficult to honor the ordinary experiences of the moment; we habitually want to highlight peak experiences. Yet the truth is that every experience, even the most mundane, offers the opportunity for deeper realization and greater clarity. We would be kinder and truer to ourselves if we honored each time we heard our hearts sing, or were aware of a deeper quietness within, or responded to a pull from deep inside. Stopping our minds from creating a familiar drama may not seem as glitzy as seeing divine lights, yet that moment is perhaps as significant to our unfolding as our first experience of nothingness or the longed-for merging with all of creation.

Discovering Ourselves in the Flow

Before the body, before the story, before the name

Beyond the mind's attempt to find or explain

Before the breath, beyond the sense of pleasure
or of pain

And after death, and after death, I am

Within the heart, the whole and part of everything
I see

Behind the eyes, beyond disguise, reflecting me

At the silent core, and yet before, phenomena began

And after it, and after it, I am

a portion of "I Am" by Kirtana

Identification and Attachments

WHO ARE WE, REALLY? Do we really want to know? The good news is that if we really want to know, we can discover the truth of our own being. To explore the truth of our existence means to gradually bring into awareness our presence on the wave. Once in this awareness, what eventually gets discarded is our fantasy of who we are, and what unfolds is the realization of the truth of our being.

Throughout time, sages have been suggesting that seekers explore what they are not as a way of making more apparent that which they are. We are not the personas we present, the beliefs we identify with, or the concepts and ideas we hold dear. We are not the roles in our lives—mother, lover, friend, or career—yet we identify ourselves as such. We are not the achievements we strive for, even though our personalities may use them as an indicator of worth and enjoy basking in the accolades they may produce. Illusion feeds our seemingly endless identification with who we think we are. Some of these identifications are looming and obvious. Others are hidden and very subtle.

We may want to embrace the idea that we are not who we think we are, yet we have been conditioned to believe otherwise. The transition necessitates a gradual letting go of our misidentifications in order to know who we really are and return to that from which we came. As we dissolve our identification with "what we are not," apparent to behold is "that which is" in all its infinite glory. Who we truly are is closer than our minds, our bodies, or our personalities. Who we truly are is absolutely perfect with nothing to fix or change.

As awareness of the wave expands, we begin to question our identification with our minds and their ideas and concepts, our personalities with their elaborate defense systems, and our bodies with our perceptions of their perfections and imperfections. These identifications block our ability to really know who we are. Questioning our assumptions is an important signal that we have opened ourselves to discovering the truth of our own beings.

The shift in identification may move through several stages. Initially, a questioning arises that shakes the solidity of conditioned misconceptions of who we think we are. While involved in the questioning, a deep inner resonating emerges. Increasingly, we experience the silence of the heart and our presence with the wave. We discover that our identity is shifting from our minds, bodies, personalities, and accomplishments to something deeper within. While *being* in awareness of the wave, our openness and vibration readies us for an experience of who we truly are. This experience can be coupled with a discovery of the identity of Essence. The process does not end here, but continues with a deepening surrender to *being* one with Essence.

We have a tendency to identify with our bodies, minds, personalities, and actions. All of these misidentifications interplay with the others, yet for the purposes of exploration we will seek to examine them somewhat separately.

We Are Not Our Bodies

Most of us would say that we know we are not our bodies. It seems true that something remains after the body dies. We experience something deeper than these surface bodies,

whether we call that something our Soul, Self, or God. Whatever we choose to label Essence, we have a deepening awareness that the truth of who we are is not the physical form.

On a more subtle level, we may smile at our identification
with the body as we notice ourselves standing in front of the
mirror primping, hoping the extra pounds don't show or
wanting a certain someone to find us attractive. We live in a
culture in which an inordinate amount of energy is focused on
how one looks. Consequently, we have internalized what we
have gleaned from others regarding our appearance, and we
have defined ourselves by these deeply ingrained imprints. "I
am pretty," "I am too tall," and "I am too old" are all beliefs
that usually point out in one way or another we are either too
much or not enough.

Certainly all of us identify ourselves by gender. We find
ourselves in a human body of one or the other sex, and we
probably enjoy our maleness or femaleness. In addition, we
are attached to certain concepts relating to gender-specific
qualities and behaviors. Certainly some are anatomical, but
most gender-related concepts have been socialized into our
minds. Society provides an incentive to continually update our
definitions from previously ingrained stereotypes of what it is
to be a man or woman. Yet most people are deeply attached
to ideas regarding what a man or woman "should be." These
concepts come wrapped in packaging of cultural heritage.

We not only identify ourselves in terms of our gender and
attractiveness, but by our capacity to function sexually. In
these bodies, but mostly in our minds, lies an urge to express
our sexuality. Sexuality is a powerful agenda-filled force.
Therefore, our sexual identification is laden with misidentification. When we compare ourselves to these gender criteria,
we often come up short. What can emerge is yet another
version of "not enough," none of it having anything to do with
who we really are.

Until we let it go, our identification with our bodies is destined to cause us much grief. It is not who we truly are. Yet we remain living in this world of relative reality with concepts regarding what is attractive, how one should look, and the meaning of sexuality. As we begin to release these beliefs, they have less and less authority over the way we see our bodies or identify ourselves, and less and less influence over the way in which we perceive others. We experience a certain freedom in releasing ourselves from these body identifications and all the suffering we inflict upon ourselves because of them. The imprinting is deep, thus the shift in identification from these surface bodies to the silence within may be gradual.

Each of us is pure perfection, pure consciousness. Consciousness has molded itself into form to create these bodies. With our minds, we have twisted consciousness into patterns of beliefs, attitudes, and defenses resulting in chronic body tension and further distortion of truth. All of this effort is a highly creative attempt of our bodies and personalities to construct a defense against feeling vulnerable.

Our bodies are the exquisite vehicles in which we are to live this life. Through inhabiting them, we may come to know the truth that we seek. As we become clearer and cleaner, the knot of misidentification slowly untwists itself. As this unraveling occurs, it allows the flow of the wave within to seep from our inner being to the surface of our bodies. We become more radiant. The happiness that we truly are permeates our bodies more and more. As our radiance blooms, our bodies become a purer instrument of Essence.

To facilitate the free flow of the wave throughout the body, we can soften many of the blocks, the chronic tensions and distortions of consciousness that have been created. The ways in which we have misconstrued our identity, the false concepts and beliefs we hold, as well as chronically held tension from traumatic events in our lives, have created these distortions. Body-oriented psychotherapies have long held the tenet that our life story can be told in how we hold chronic tension in our bodies. When one works with this tension, memories and feelings often emerge related to the events that first gave birth to the muscular holding creating the tension. By releasing the memories and allowing the feelings to have their expression, the chronic tension dissipates.

Several Eastern spiritual traditions have married spiritual work and body movement. Yoga, Tai Chi, Dahn Hak, and Chi Gung are but a few of the forms that increase the flow of chi or life energy throughout the body. Most communities have an abundance of individuals who practice some form of body-work. Many massage therapists and healers, to name a few, are as interested in the spiritual unfolding of their clients as they are in their physical health.

Not surprisingly, these areas of chronic tension are the same places where the body is susceptible to disease and illness. But what has been held in the body can be released and find expression. Moving our bodies in freeform dance or letting our expression loose through painting, music, or writing are all ways to unburden our bodies. As we clear out the distortions and debris that obstruct our expression, consciousness is then freed to flow through our bodies in all its radiance.

These bodies we call ours are the temples of the beloved Essence, and as such, we can either treat them as a sacred space or we can abuse them. Pretty clearly, we have that choice. For example, we may be so consumed by an addiction for alcohol that we bring destruction to our internal organs, to say nothing about bringing havoc to our personal lives. It is a day for celebration when the resolve arises to end addictions that abuse our bodies and our psyches. At that point, to berate ourselves for the damage done is counterproductive. The best choice we can make is to come to love what is, to

love and accept our bodies and personalities as perfect
vessels for our unfolding.

Some people hold the tenet that any illness of the body is
of our own creation. From the common perspective of relative
reality, such a view has unfortunately caused many people to
blame themselves for their cancer or chronic illness. In absolute reality, this is all our creation, the Self is the author of this
movie, and certain adversity may very well be present in our
lives as a vehicle for our unfolding. Yet thinking we know why
someone has a particular illness seems to me nothing but
speculation and personal projection.

In addition, some people enter this world into bodies that
create great challenges. They may be missing a certain capacity that usually comes as standard equipment. While they can
be assisted with whatever knowledge current medical tech-
niques provide, ultimately, they too have the choice to come
to love what is. Someone who has come to *be* with such an
adversity in a way that radiates his or her true identity loves
what is and inspires all of us. The way that we all choose to *be*
with our own unique challenges is the ever-present opportunity for our unfolding. Again, the best choice for our unfolding
is to *be* with what is in such a way that we deepen our love and
acceptance for both the body and the personality while
coming to realize that our true identity is neither.

We Are Not Our Minds

MANY PEOPLE IDENTIFY WITH THEIR MINDS. They perceive themselves to be what they think. They may perceive themselves to
be one who is clever or witty or wise. Their intellectual ventures have been fruitful and integral to their sense of worth.
Others retreat to the world of the mind after deducing it to be
safer than their feeling world. This is particularly true of people

who, at an early age, began to fear that their feelings would overwhelm them and were clever enough to discover that using their minds would help keep a shaky world in control. In their fright, they may have frozen feelings in their bodies, so diminishing the flow of energy that they have a look of deadness. These chronic tensions that hold the stored feelings in place need to be freed in order for their natural radiance to emerge again. To venture into their feelings is a courageous act as they do not trust them, but rather have learned to trust their thoughts. They believe that who they are is what they think.

Most of us identify with our minds. Lest you think you have escaped this identification, watch yourself the next time someone disagrees with a concept or idea about which you are passionate. If you find yourself taking that individual's rejection of your idea personally, you have discovered one of your identifications. We have been so strongly conditioned in our educational systems to validate our worth by our minds' ability to come up with the right answers! We are not our minds. Because our ideas may be rejected does not mean we are rejected.

Just because we think something does not make it true. This is blatantly obvious to all of us, yet we continue to seek to understand the mysteries of the universe through our minds. This cannot be done. The shifting of mental concepts does not break the illusion of relative reality. We may change from one spiritual concept to the next. Our belief in these concepts will not alter absolute reality. Just because we may want truth to take a certain form does not make it so. Really grasping that these minds we identify with are relatively useless in expanding our understanding of the most important questions of our existence is very difficult for many of us. We attach ourselves to our beliefs and hold them dear while taking credit for our mind's understanding.

One of our biggest fears is that we might "lose our minds." Actually, what gets lost as we unfold is our trust in the reality of our thoughts and our identification with the workings of our minds. Our minds are an essential part of our bodies. Our intellect is an exquisite mechanism essential for our functioning in this relative reality. Our minds are not the enemy. Only our identification with our minds must loosen and dissolve. This identification enables them to be the emperors of our lives. But as the mind gives way to the true knowing of the heart, it becomes a servant rather than the controlling force in our lives.

In the interplay between the mind and the personality, the mind becomes a defensive tool for the personality. The defense mechanisms we use to strengthen or protect our self-image are plays of the mind. We use our minds to deny or bury something we do not want to face. We use our intellect to spiritualize something we do not want to feel. We use our thoughts to create stories regarding other people's thoughts, feelings, and motivations, and then we believe the projections we have created. We may be sensitive enough to have picked up some clues, but we can never truly know another. Just attempting to get to know our own personality is difficult enough. As our faith in our projections diminishes, we gradually spin fewer stories about others.

Not only do we no longer trust our projections, we also no longer trust the stories we spin regarding possible future events in our lives. Any version of, "If I do this, she or he will do that," seems erroneous and a waste of time.

One definition of anxiety is living in the future. In the process of decreasing our trust in our projections, we make our lives less anxious. Similarly, we invest less energy in reliving past events to the tune of, "I should have done this or not said that." There are other verses to this song, but the main melody is familiar to us all. Even reliving past moments of great beauty takes us away from the beauty of the present moment. Gradually, our minds stop taking off on these "trips." When the mind is reined in, we are open to experience the ever-present wonders of the now.

The super-ego is the mind's mythical entity that is the keeper of all those "shoulds and shouldn'ts," "dos and don'ts." Some of us have lived much of our lives under the tyranny of the many "shoulds." We may well have the habit of participating in an internal dialog of our own creation that is so negative we would not tolerate such a conversation with anyone else. The rampant internal put-downs are often directed at aspects of our personalities and, very often, at our own minds. To call ourselves "dummies" for forgetting something is perhaps a mild example. Each of us has a whole barrage of the super-ego's favorite put-downs.

As we become gentler with ourselves, our tyrannical keeper begins to soften and our abusive inner dialog becomes more supportive. We can catch our mind midstream in put-down dialog and stop, no longer willing to abuse ourselves. Consequently, we less frequently berate ourselves for not living up to the super-ego's imagined ideals. Gradually the expectations change and the dialog becomes more supportive. In the process, we come to love ourselves more deeply, even as we shake the foundation of identification with our personality. The knot of misidentification begins to loosen, allowing for a fuller flow of Essence.

We Are Not Our Personalities

WHEN WE SAY WE KNOW PEOPLE, we usually mean we recognize their bodies and are acquainted with their personalities. We do the same with ourselves. In this relative reality, we think that to know ourselves is to become intimate with our person-alities and to understand both our stories and the effect that certain chapters have had on our lives.

The labels we attach to ourselves—incest victim, abuser, divorced man, ex-con, golf-pro, former Miss America—increase our identification with who we are not. The labels relate only to paragraphs or perhaps even chapters within this story we call a life. We further identify ourselves by the ethnic groups we belong to and the culture of those groups. To expand the list of identifications, we include the roles we play in our families, such as parent, child, grandparent, or spouse; or in the larger society, such as psychologist, painter, or musician. Our concept of self-worth is attached to these roles. The perception that we *are* these labels is the glue that at-taches us to the illusion of relative reality, thus hindering our perception of absolute reality. While on a psychological level, our emotions, attitudes, and behaviors cannot be ignored, we can place so much emphasis in getting to know our personali-ties that we never go deeper to find out who we truly are.

We imagine ourselves to be a personality. As long as that perception is firmly held, we have an inevitably strong invest-ment in protecting our sense of identity. Who we truly are needs no protection. Who we imagine ourselves to be surely does. Over our lifetime, we have developed intricate patterns of defensive behavior. Our personalities are identified with numerous ideas of how we "are not enough," buffered by identification with characteristics we have termed "assets." When we perceive that the assets outweigh the liabilities, we say we have a strong self-concept. When this is reversed, we say we need to build self-esteem. Wouldn't it be more truthful to become aware of who we really are?

If we just take a minute to investigate some perceived "not okay" aspect of our personality or one in which we take great pride, we can discover all the creative ways we have con-

structed to keep from feeling the pain of our perceived vulnerability. Our experience is that we must protect ourselves from
the ever-present possibility that either an asset or a liability
will be attacked. Since our identities are married to our
personalities, we are left with no choice but to keep at bay
those aspects of ourselves we perceive to not be okay and to
protect our investment in those characteristics for which we
take pride. Maintaining and carrying that baggage takes
tremendous effort. One begins to enjoy the relief as the
burdens, one by one, are put down.

As we entertain the possibility that our sense of self is a
misconception, the need to defend its constructs softens.
Many of our patterns of behavior had their inception in our
childhood. The same can be said for most of our attitudes and
beliefs. A sense of compassion naturally develops for the child
we once were. It took great creativity to develop such elaborate patterns of defensive behavior.

I am suggesting we take our patterns into our hearts and
embrace them, giving them the unconditional love of a good
parent. The ideal parent distinguishes between the child and
what he or she does. None of us had ideal parents or other
ideal adult role models in our world, and thus, we may have
only partially internalized this ability to see others and ourselves with unconditional love.

We have the capacity to give ourselves unconditional love
because who we truly are is unconditional love. As we expand
our moment-to-moment awareness of being the wave, we
open access to an endless supply of unconditional love. The
only courage necessary is a willingness to attend continually
to the call of our deepest knowing, the gentle and tender pull
home from the core of our beings. The glorious fringe benefit
is that our hearts expand and we live our lives with increasing
compassion for all.

As we treat ourselves with love, the rigidities of our bodies and personalities soften and begin to allow other submerged blocks to emerge into awareness. If we take our hands off the thoughts and feelings that arrive and just let them be bathed in loving gentleness, they will soften. Slowly, as their defensive function no longer has a purpose, the patterns begin to dissolve. The love from within makes the defense unnecessary.

This means being in the moment with our feelings in what John deRuiter calls "gentle okay-ness." Whatever patterns emerge, they are okay. To *be* in the moment means to let ourselves see, to not deny or judge, to not try to fix the patterns or make them go away. If we let ourselves truly experience what is here in the moment, if we let that experience fully inhabit our physical, mental, and emotional bodies, it will wash through our physical beings. This is surrendering to ourselves.

To not resist such a cleansing goes against our conditioning. Our bodies are exquisite instruments with muscles that have been trained to hold on. These bodies have attempted to take care of us at a tremendous price, that of chronic tension. As a result of life experience, we have developed what have now become automatic physical responses to perceived threats.

For example, we may have learned as a child it was best not to cry through hearing the parental injunction, "Don't cry or I will give you something to cry about." When the impulse to cry arises in our adult life, we may discover a lump in our throat as those muscles tighten to protect us and keep the sobs from surfacing. If, however, we let ourselves really cry, then our sadness has an expression. Once we begin to allow the tears, a historic fear of reprisal may momentarily arise. We may also be afraid that we will never stop crying, but, as the sadness washes through, what we actually discover is a sense of relief and a relaxation. The chronic tension in our bodies begins to relax. After repeated opportunities to cry, the wisdom of the body readjusts itself, and the muscles no longer automatically tighten as sadness starts to erupt into tears.

Embracing fear is a courageous act. We are so afraid that going deeply into any feeling might be the end of us. Actually, this is true, but not in the way we fear. A common fear is that, if we go deeply into our pain, it will overwhelm us. But, if we really let the pain, fear, laughter, or whatever envelope us, we discover it moves right on through. It has a life, and then it dissolves. We emerge refreshed, often having released a primitive pattern.

Gradually, we begin to trust the process and become less defensive, having realized that whatever we experience will pierce us and move through. When we don't judge or stop our minds as we find condemnation emerging, we experience less of a need for defense. If we don't assume an aspect of our personalities needs fixing, it has an opportunity to have its life and dissolve. Increasingly, our behavior is less impulsive. We can observe thoughts, feelings, and attitudes without judgment and notice less of a need to act them out. We can dare to be open, expansive, and vulnerable.

How much of our physical appearance, our susceptibility to diseases, and our personality traits are a result of nature or nurture has long been debated. The phenomenon of identical twins has enabled us to see how much our body's physical appearance is determined by our genes. Yet, there is a less wide acceptance of the impact of heredity on personality.

Animal breeders have long honored the impact of the gene pool on personality traits. An accomplished dog breeder can tell you which young members of a litter will be aggressive and dominant and which will be more passive, which will be a good companion and which will have difficulty making attachments. If one stands at a hospital nursery window and observes, some of these same traits are apparent in human babies.

Making peace with the fact that we may not have been born with musical talent is easier to accept than the fact that we may not have a strong assertiveness, especially if family or peers hold this trait in high esteem. Yet to take responsibility for some aspects of our personalities is about as useful as taking responsibility for the size of our nose.

That our environment shapes our personalities, particularly as it relates to attitudes and patterns of defensive behavior, is also very clear. Becoming acquainted with our personal stories has been important for many of us. Now, as adults, we are able to see that many of the hurtful things said to us as children regarding our personalities were taken in whole and believed. The reality is that most were not true and only the perception of another.

If we are not introspective and attuned to the feelings, attitudes, beliefs, and defensive patterns of our personalities, then understanding how we get caught and distracted becomes more difficult, if not impossible. Thus, we remain captured by our patterns. Sometimes, seeing denial in our fellow inmates in this illusory prison called conditioned existence is easier than seeing it in ourselves. Most of us could conjure up an example of a person in our lives who is blatantly predictable in succumbing to particular behavior patterns that distract them from being aware of whom they really are. But can we notice the same tendency in ourselves?

After a time, attachment to one's story is counterproductive. What is important is to stay in the moment, rather than to attach one's mind to the past, especially if the story is one we know well and are revisiting for the hundredth time. To continue to feed the seeming reality of the story is once again to identify with being a character in the play. We can easily get stuck in replaying the story of the traumatic events of our lives. We have attended to the story long enough. To replay the story serves only to keep the identification alive.

Not only have I been a psychotherapist, I spent many years in psychotherapy myself. My identity was connected both with my profession and with my personal story. At some point, I became aware of an increasing quietness inside, and I did not know whether to attribute that to my daily practice of meditation or to my psychotherapy. My guess was that it was a combination of both.

Eventually, while attending a faculty meeting at a psychological institute in New York City, I made what I was afraid would be greeted as a heretical statement. Attending were seasoned colleagues who dedicated themselves to a particular form of body-oriented psychotherapy. My comment was that I had come to feel that the essential ingredient in a client's psychotherapy was not the use of any particular modality, but the therapist's unconditional love. Once clients could provide unconditional love for themselves, therapy was no longer needed. I was surprised at the affirmation with my stance.

Eventually, however, I no longer sought out therapy. I became less identified with my story, and my meditation became being in silence. About that time, I resigned from the faculty and closed my practice. Something was pulling me deeper. As I discovered myself on the wave, the importance of unconditional love revealed itself as truth.

We Are Not What We Do

THE MOST POWERFUL IDENTIFICATION most people have is connected to what they do. So much of our identity is related to a feeling of accomplishment or lack thereof. In Western culture, strong emphasis is placed on our achievements. Our sense of worth is deeply connected with doing, accomplishing, or being of service.

As adults, one of the first things we are asked upon meeting someone is, "What is it that you do?" At best, this question is designed to illicit information as to our interests. Historically, the question has been painted with the brush of a status indicator. We have all known people, who live their lives at a fast pace, to seek yet another accolade as they progress through some corporate structure. The term "rat race" comes from the psychological experiments of running rats through mazes. Indeed this is what life can look and feel like when achievement is our primary or only goal.

Inherent in this striving are the compromises made in order to meet a personal agenda or to support an agenda of an organization. At times, the price of these compromises seems too high as we feel a warp in our personal integrity. Diminished are the moment-to-moment pleasures of life. The resultant stresses on our bodies can be hefty. The trophy never proves any of the things we hope it will prove to ourselves. No trophy ever will.

As we think about the people we have known in our lives—not read about, but known—only a few really stand out. Chances are very high that they stand out not because of what they have done, but by their manner of *being*. There presence of *being* is what impacted our lives. What activity they were engaged in did not matter. What did matter was their way of *being* with that activity. What they were about had a simplicity, a true honesty, and a heart-centeredness. They knew what gave meaning to their lives. The agendas, the striving for affirmations, no longer held significance. A true joy of *being* was present in whatever they were doing.

Many awakened people on this planet live quiet lives, unnoticed by those around them as anyone remarkable. The truth is that, as we become more evolved, we experience ourselves as more and more ordinary. We no longer need to accomplish something fantastic or have peak experiences, because what were once extra-ordinary moments are now ordinary.

What were once the trophies of this life no longer seem alluring. Any sense of specialness quietly dissolves along with any need to be somebody. Being nobody is our heart's love. The reality is that there really is no body, no individual separate from consciousness itself, and no one body is more special than any other. To hear this is very threatening to many, as their identity and worth are deeply connected with their roles and accomplishments. One needs to be very gentle with oneself when the threat to one's specialness shows itself.

As we more frequently discover ourselves as one with the wave of creation, we discover that it flows whether we are consciously aware of it or not. Our lives unfold. We can be in harmony with that evolution or struggle against it, but the wave flows on. In one moment we may seek out an astrologer or a psychic to discover what is to happen next in our lives, and then, in the next moment we are sure that we are the architects of our own destiny. And we never notice the discrepancy!

The reality is that not the mind, the personality, nor the body is the doer. Consciousness is the doer. As all false structures of identification begin to unwind within our form, flowing as this consciousness, this Essence becomes easier and easier. Familiar distractions have less of an appeal, and we are less drawn to go against the flow. Essence can find clearer expression through our minds, bodies, and personalities. Our forms are freer just to be expressions of *all that is*, unencumbered in its radiance. Essence can utilize the mind, personality, and body to express and experience itself. The clearer and cleaner, the less twisted we are, the freer we are to experience the wave of creation as it flows through our beings.

Dissolving Patterns

As WE DISSOLVE THE BLOCKS to our awareness, our presence as
the wave becomes more readily apparent. What does dissolving mean? First, it means to honestly notice the block. Second, it means to gently embrace ourselves with unconditional,
nonjudgmental love. To "notice" means to attend with absolute honesty. Such attention is a lifetime commitment to
vigilance, the resolve to no longer abide in self-delusion. The
willingness for honesty can pierce and penetrate any delusion.
To notice takes a willingness to really see what *is*, rather than
what we *want* to be. Our fear is that we will discover we are as
vile as we are afraid we are. This is, of course, an identification
with our super-ego's judgments. Yet, if we allow honesty to
cut right through the patterns and judgments, what emerges is
the gentle, unconditional, loving of our core being.

Perhaps we notice that certain behaviors are defense
mechanisms that close us off from being in the moment with
an experience. To dissolve a pattern means to notice what is
taking place, not judge it, take our hands off it, and be gently
accepting of ourselves. As a thought or feeling is brought into
loving awareness, it is experienced simply as it is in the
moment, and then it dissolves. The thoughts and agenda
behaviors are fed when we attack, judge, or take a hands-on
approach to changing a pattern. In doing so, we only further
identify with that which we wish to dissolve.

Denial is strengthened by self-judgment, creating a vicious
cycle of self-deception. To notice and be brutally honest with
oneself in terms of acknowledging the blocks is important.
Then we need lovingly to let them be okay without any attempt to change. The blocks will soften and dissolve in
response to love. Softening our hearts and bodies happens in

the presence of love. To be patiently, unconditionally loving with ourselves is to be in harmony with Essence. Essence is unconditional love.

The patterns are endless, or so it seems as one dissolves and another emerges to take its place. That is how it is. But, eventually, there is a sense of ourselves as being cleaner and clearer. The initial gross patterns are replaced by finer ones until, eventually, we are attending to those that others might not even notice. Yet, we know, because we are aware that something is just not quite in harmony. This process of unfolding takes place with both moments of great clarity and periods of napping. With attention, the naps become shorter and less frequent and the clarity brighter and more vibrant.

A second implied ingredient important for dissolving patterns is that of non-judgment. Much of our self-judgment is some variation on "not being enough." We have internalized the concept of not being enough along with stringent concepts of right and wrong, good and bad. We hypnotize ourselves with these perceptions, causing ourselves great suffering. None of it is real.

The quickest way to entrench a pattern of behavior is to judge it, thus creating the necessity to strengthen our habitual defenses. The rationalizations, denials, and projections become stronger. Most of these patterns of behavior are so automatic that they go unnoticed.

The behaviors are not who we are. How could who we truly are not be good enough? It's not possible. When we remember that we are not our behaviors, thoughts, beliefs, or attitudes, we give them permission to surface, where we have the opportunity to look at each one in the light of love. As we become less self-judging and more lovingly okay, our defenses melt. Our bodies, minds, and personalities become more open to be an expression of who we truly are.

Life's events have a way of occasionally hitting us upside the head with a two-by-four, clamoring for our attention. The gift of these times is that we are forced to look at the behaviors, attitudes, and beliefs that consistently cause us suffering. They may once have served a purpose, but now they create havoc for us and possibly others. Such times often provide an opportunity to see in bold relief that what we identify with is what creates our misery and suffering.

Our partner finds another, and we experience grief at the loss, a feeling that clamors for expression and release from the body. Accompanying the feelings are the mind's misperceptions that we are the jilted one, the abandoned one, the loser, the one who was not enough. We have a choice in each moment to identify with these misperceptions or remember who we really are. A question such as, "Who is the loser?" may help trigger an awareness that we are once again caught in misidentification. For who we truly are is not a loser, and when we bring our identification to our true identity, we will no longer feel like one.

Perhaps the pattern is more ordinary. One of mine has been an impatience that sometimes surfaces in the checkout line of the grocery store when I am behind someone who takes out their checkbook and begins writing a check after their total has been rung up. When I notice my impatience, a helpful question is, "Who is this *somebody* who feels they have rights here?" Gradually, the question is no longer needed. To notice my impatience is all that is necessary to remind myself of who I am, usually followed with a smile at the tenacity of such an inconsequential pattern. We all have such ordinary and equally tenacious patterns. All are gold for remembering and re-identifying with our true self.

Whichever misperception surfaces, we can be sure it has been well entrenched in our personality. We need to be gently okay with the comings and goings of each misperception. Some of these false identities can be respected for their tenacity as they hang on and play frequent reruns, while others quickly dissolve in the light of truth. When we use these life events to bring clarity and release old ways, we can indeed see them as gifts. We are abundantly provided for by grace. Suffering becomes replaced by gratitude, yet externally nothing may have changed.

Most of us have at one time or another noticed how easily we fall into familiar roles and patterns of behavior and mis-identification while with our families of origin. The stronger the relationship or the more historic, the more easily we get pulled into familiar roles or into another's drama. Once caught in their seeming reality, we have lost awareness.

We need to be gentle with ourselves. The gentler we are, the more quickly we will discover we have been snared yet again and simply withdraw from the role. The next time, or maybe the time after that, awareness will enable us to avoid becoming seduced into being a character in our own or someone else's drama. However, for whatever period of time we lose awareness of the knower and identify with our minds and personalities, we are once again captured in the drama. Once involved, our personalities play out our entrenched patterns, and we remain susceptible to any suffering the dramas create.

Dramas take place on the stage of judgment, both of others and ourselves. To chide ourselves is counterproductive. We need to be gentle with ourselves. These patterns of thoughts, behaviors, and attitudes are a substantial part of our conditioning, including the temptation to chide ourselves.

Patterns melt in the warmth of unconditional love. Our true nature as Essence can immediately be rediscovered. Dramas evaporate when viewed by the knower, who is eternally steadfast in awareness of who we truly are. Through the eyes of the divine knower, we see that the drama is not about us.

When we regain our footing on the wave, we behold a fresh discovery of our true identity. Once again, we can see the actors, including ourselves, with compassion. The events of the drama, no matter how painful, are perceived as a gift. We have given ourselves another opportunity to honestly see a pattern, and another opportunity to strengthen our realization of who we really are.

Perhaps what got played out was a rerun of an old script. One more time we played people who perceived themselves as outsiders looking in, or perhaps we perceived ourselves as lacking some essential attribute others had. The storyline calls for a belief that we are not enough or we would not be on the outside, and the drama continues to get played out from that erroneous vantage point.

Slowly, as we sever our identification with what we are not, what is real has more clarity and depth, and we begin to live from an awareness of our true identity. Eventually, we can sense our figurative feet firmly rooted in absolute reality. Our identity is grounded in the truth of absolute reality while still experiencing and enjoying this relative reality. We are able to take off the colored glasses of "not enough" and seriously inquire, "*Who* is it who is not enough?" This clarity of vision becomes a gentle reminder of who we truly are.

We make the assumption that many events in our lives happen due to some failure on our parts. We could have; we should have; we ought to have done this or that; all the ways we have of torturing ourselves. These beliefs also assume that we have choice.

I am not sure how much choice we really have. I have no expectation that I will know the answer to that question while in this form, and that is fine. But I am certain that we have a choice as to how we perceive any of the events of our lives. We have a choice in any given moment to be honest and to tell the truth to ourselves.

We then have the choice to live our truth or not. Our awareness of our deep connection with all of creation will gently guide us home. That tug from within may be the angel that is nudging us toward home and away from false identifications and attachments that distract us from what we know. However, the choice is ours as to whether we go with the flow or continue to swim across the current in another direction.

A belief that all we have to do is hang out on the raft and unfolding will take care of itself is a misconception, a rationalization of the mind. It is a misconception that all we need to do is be around a powerful enlightened being, and our exposure to their state will take us home without any effort on our part.

Our unfolding may be perceived as a combination of self-awareness and grace. The desire to live in truth is paramount. The only effort required is to be in the moment and to pay attention, to honestly notice, accompanied by gentle okayness with whatever emerges.

Grace is not something any of us earn. The grace that permeates our lives is a gift of Essence. The openness of our hearts and our capacity to receive grace enables us to be sustained by its bounty.

Leaving
the Dream
Behind

Meet me where the river meets the sea
Naked now, innocent and free
Beloved, I have been waiting throughout time
To welcome you into these arms of mine

Come without a thought
About what's been or what's in store
Leave the world of mind behind you
Like sandals by the shore

from "Meet Me" by Kirtana

Our Myths of Realization

ONE OF THE GREAT PARADOXES of our spiritual evolution is that no one becomes enlightened. At that juncture, one discovers there is no you or me to be enlightened. Thus the great cosmic joke! Being a human being is to have a life full of such paradoxes.

The term self-realization is often defined as knowing who one is, while enlightenment is defined as knowing the identity of God or Essence. For some people, these understandings come simultaneously. For others, they are separate realizations. Some of us may have initially thought that either of these realizations would come in a big-bang experience, and everything would then change, preferably with no involvement on our part. With our Western ears, we have heard some Eastern teachers say that all suffering would stop (we assumed that also meant pain!). Our minds would stop. We would be beyond emotion and would have the powers we had somehow been led to believe would be ours once we merged with God. If we were one with God, we would be all knowing, all loving, and all powerful too.

To know that we are one with Essence does not mean we merge with a preconceived concept of the absolute.

I grew up believing in an all-knowing, all-powerful and loving God and assumed enlightened teachers were also the embodiment of these traits. Initially, it seemed to me that to become enlightened was to become my concept of God.

One evening in a meditation satsang, Swami Chidvalasanda commented on a letter she had received from a follower who was a scientist. He assumed she understood everything he understood about his very specialized scientific area. He perceived that as an enlightened being, she was the embodiment of his concept of an all-knowing God. He is not unique in his misunderstanding.

We may not have heard the reality that realization is not a final experience, only that our understanding unfolds and deepens. We did not hear that an experience is just that, an experience. Liberation is not an automatic or instantaneous result of any experience.

A friend shared with me an occurrence in which he perceived everything as being "light." He saw everything as a blaze of glory for quite a period of time. He calls it his heavenly experience. He knew he was this light. Yes, the experience changed his concept of reality. Such experiences are illuminating. His understanding deepened. However, his impulsiveness continued to create stress and drama in his life.

One needs to be willing to surrender one's greed for always wanting more of whatever entices, be it more money or more sex or even more enlightenment. It takes willingness for stark honesty to see one's behavior and then enough self-love to be able to hold what one discovers in gentle okay-ness. Stark honesty is essential, as it is very easy for the mind to rationalize and spiritualize our behavior. "Spirit's will" has been used as a rationale for many a distraction. Only stark honesty accompanied by loving acceptance allows us to soften and surrender that which has been a distraction.

The fruit of these realization experiences emerges as we continue to surrender to being the truth we now understand. What is crucial is to embody the understanding in such a way that our manner of being in the present has been altered. This means *being* that which we know.

Can't Know Until You Know

SOME SEEKERS HAVE A CONCEPT of what they think self-realization or enlightenment is and how it should look in another.
Thus, they want realization to fit their image. To believe you
understand something you have yet to experience is bound to
create a filter that may block the discovery of truth.

These suppositions regarding realization seem to take two
predictable forms. The first is to so glorify enlightenment that
no living person can possibly fit the definition—only a very
few enlightened masters of the past. Had one been present
when these past masters were alive, they probably would not
have fit the definition either. A person who so glorifies enlightenment never finds a teacher who fits their mold and therefore
who is good enough for them to trust to be their guide. This is
basically a stance emanating from not trusting oneself enough
to have discernment.

I recently heard an American, who is a Hindu swami,
comment on the words purportedly spoken by Jesus while he
was suffering on the cross. Jesus asks his God why he has
forsaken him. The swami's comment was that, at this point,
Jesus had lost his enlightened state. Earlier I had heard him
make a similar statement regarding Jesus' possible anger when
he banished the moneychangers from the temple. If I understood the swami correctly, his comments were an example of
creating a standard for the enlightened state that necessitates
surrendering one's humanness.

To me, such criteria perpetuate the idealized definition of
enlightenment. Yes, we can have enlightening experiences that
create a change in the way we perceive this world and ourselves. *Being* the embodiment of that which we have come to

understand is a process that ever deepens. There is no goal to be reached. We do not need a standard of perfection by which to compare ourselves or for which to strive. We can only be present, moment-to-moment, in awareness and honest noticing, all the while being gentle with our humanness or occasional naps. There is no final destination. What has no beginning also has no end.

Many years ago, while attending a Good Friday service, I heard a renowned Protestant theologian speak about the words of Jesus on the cross, "My God, my God, why have you forsaken me?" (Mark 15: 34) as gift to all of us. He suggested that, in calling out to his God, Jesus had shared his humanness. This great being was in a human body.

When that body was racked with pain, Jesus may or may not have temporarily lost his sense of connection. If he did so, it does not in the least detract from the life and teachings of this man. In fact, one can perceive it as an enhancement. His words can be seen in such a way as to give us permission to honor and hold our humanness in great love. They can also be used to underscore our need for noticing and being aware when we have temporarily lost our awareness. While in a human body, all of us may have such moments of forgetting. At those moments of noticing our forgetfulness, we may cry out to our God, wondering where the divine presence is, or we may have another means of rediscovering the flow. For me, that means is to return my attention to the depths of my heart.

In addition, if we believe that there have only ever been one or two enlightened people on this planet, then we take ourselves off the hook by a beautiful play of the mind. One can easily rationalize that one could not possibly be like Jesus or Buddha, Therefore, the individual doesn't have to really commit to this unfolding. This rationale is not only a copout; it is also a block to knowing the truth of one's own being.

A second form that myths of realization may take is also an idealized concept of realization, but it creates the opposite distortion—that of perceiving whatever a teacher does in such a way as to fit a glorified image. The idealized filter through which one sees a teacher is so distorted that it necessitates a spiritual rationale for all the teacher's behavior. Discernment necessitates an openness to allow for the humanness in our teachers. Enlightened and self-realized people are in human bodies, susceptible to their humanness. In addition, by creating such an idealized mental image, liberation seems even more unattainable.

The truth is we do not know what realization or enlightenment is until we know. The words themselves are even confusing. Liberation is not something we can achieve; it will happen in its own time. First, an important ingredient is to let go of preconceived ideas about what self-realization or liberation is. These preconceptions just get in our way. We don't need to know, and the truth is that we don't know until we know. The openness to not knowing is a key to liberation.

Second, we seem to have a choice in any moment to cooperate with the unfolding or not. Cooperation is being open in each moment. It is not being on a quest. When we stop the search, we can just rest and be the embodiment of our current understanding. In this human form, that is all that is truly possible both before and after any peak experience. No human has yet described an end to realization.

Self-Doubt

THE SIDE EFFECT OF A PRECONCEIVED NOTION of self-realization is that we may long to know the truth, but doubt we will discover it in this lifetime. However, many sages have said that as we come closer to having our longing fulfilled, our desire becomes more intense. Also true is that, as our desire becomes more powerful, we open access within to the experiences for which we have been pining. Many of us have experienced our desire becoming more intense.

At some time in our lives, our spiritual unfolding was important, but certainly not the most important ingredient in our lives. Almost imperceptibly, this may have changed. For many, knowing truth and being truth is their life. When the fire of love burns intensely into a deep longing for Essence, your Beloved finds you. Kirtana sings from the vantage of your Beloved, or Essence, with the words, "Beloved, I have waited throughout time to welcome you into these arms of mine." We are our Beloved's Beloved. We can have what we long for. The Beloveds can find each other and become one. Our Beloved is us.

Self-doubt is a play of the mind that can create a block to our unfolding. A major ingredient of self-doubt is false humility, which downplays whatever our current understanding may be, especially to ourselves. We can stop ourselves from venturing into any play of the mind that undercuts our trust in our capacity to continually open to truth and *be* the little bit of truth we know. Our reason for birth is to rediscover that which we all are. If doing so is what we truly want, it is there, readily available and waiting for our embrace.

Another pothole is to fall into believing that we are not worthy: "Who me? I can't possibly be good enough." Who we truly are is absolutely perfect. True, our behavior may never meet the standards of our preconceived, idealized criteria, but our Beloved will not reject us! Our minds and our personalities may, others may, but not our Beloved.

The mind and the personality forget who we are. Others may not see who we are. As long as we maintain the illusion of our imperfection, we have created a haze through which we are attempting to find our Beloved. Our radiance cannot join the Beloved's radiance as one. Remembering can become increasingly easy. The benefits in our life make it worth our attention. The pain encountered along the way helps clear out the rubble. We can find out what remains.

Flowing with the Wave

This is the nectar my living is worth
This is my purpose, my reason for birth
It was not for some future my mind could conceive
And not for the deeds my will could achieve
But only for love, only this love

from "Only This Love" by Kirtana

Heartfelt Being

A HEARTFELT LIFE IS OUR HEART'S DESIRE. It is the most delicious way to be in this world and the most courageous. Each of us experiences many moments when we have felt our existence emanating from our hearts. In those moments, our hearts feel filled to the brim, and everything has the radiance of sunshine. Those of us who are parents relished the joy of the first time we held our newborn and counted all its fingers and toes. The same joy can be found in being present with any newborn in nature.

We treasure the highs of a new love affair and want to hold on to that intoxicating feeling, yet it seems to elude us. In relationships, love deepens and grows, yet to expect the constancy of this high defies our experience. Relationships change like most everything else. Yet, when we open ourselves to a love affair with what never changes, the availability of *being* a deeper, purer love unfolds. To *be* such love in the moment-to-moment necessitates an undefended heart.

Undefended Heart

HEARTBREAK HAS BEEN OUR COMPANION and will continue to be. A heart that can be broken is a heart that can endlessly expand and be the love that is Essence. Or a cracked heart can contract, becoming hardened and more defended. A defended heart is armored against pain.

Each of us learned very early in our lives the pain of a crack in the heart. To be alive is to have heartbreak. We have a choice as to how we are with these inevitable heart ruptures.

A closed heart will find it difficult, perhaps be unwilling, to open sufficiently to allow even a glimpse of the flow of the wave within. This imprisoned heart does not protect us, but causes more suffering. One reason for armoring a heart is to protect ourselves from rejection. Such an armored heart creates a sense of isolation and loneliness. More importantly, such armoring inhibits or prevents access to our innermost core and the awareness of the wave. By defending our hearts, we cut ourselves off from the intimacy we seek both with others and with ourselves.

We can be with a depth of love that is beyond our imagining. All we need do is be in harmony with the wave. We can be the love we so desperately look for from the outside. Such a change may seem like a radical shift, and it is also possible.

To have such a transformation in our lives means having the courage to rest in an undefended heart. Such a heart can sing at any moment. Such a heart will see more deeply the joys and pain in the world. Such a heart will be continually pierced in its nakedness. The flow of the wave allows us to experience whatever is in the moment and then flows on. There is no need to either hold on to or bury any feelings or experiences. Therefore, such a heart and its body are not cluttered with remnants of traumas. The feelings are relished in the moment and then pass through. The body of such a person becomes an open temple, available for consciousness to inhabit it increasingly in a natural, untwisted form, thus creating a radiance.

As we experience ourselves as the wave, our capacity to be in our heart expands. We are aware of becoming more heart-centered, more compassionate. Gradually, we are no longer willing to defend the heart in order to keep from experiencing pain. Whatever defenses we have used to keep the pain out did not discriminate, but just depleted our emotions and deadened our bodies.

Our bodies are not constructed to feel only what we want to feel. When we armor our bodies, we create a shield with our musculature. We appear to create a safe capsule for ourselves. In actuality, we deaden our bodies and defend against all feeling. A diminished depth of joy is the compromise. We have imprisoned our hearts in a cage built of defenses. Consciousness has become twisted.

When we open the door of the cage, our hearts soar while singing our freedom song. We discover the exhilaration of flying free and unencumbered. Consciousness can untwist itself and flow freely. The experience of nakedness becomes addictive. The analogy that comes to my mind is a mild version, but may help to illustrate. If you have ever taken off your clothes and gone skinny-dipping, you know the pleasure of swimming unencumbered by clothes. The feel of the water on your skin, the freedom of no restraints, can make skinny-dipping the preferred way to swim. The feeling of nakedness is delicious.

We will not be arrested and charged with indecent exposure for having a naked heart. There is no propriety in the love affair within, no time when an undefended heart overflowing with Essence is not appropriate. Less and less frequent are the times when such innocence seems too vulnerable. Less and less do we dampen that innocence with restraints. Freedom is our song.

All of us have had to learn many ways to clothe and armor our hearts. Some wrappings are familiar. Other garments are made of such highly invisible and effective material that we may not even know we have them on. It is our personalities' belief that the presence of these defenses is mandatory for our existence. As we loosen the grip of our identification with our personalities, we open the door to allowing our buried defenses to make themselves known. The established ways in which we open and close our hearts become more familiar. Such defenses deserve to be treated with patience, gentle okay-ness, and respect for our personalities' creativity in discovering the very best way available to feel safe.

No one gives up freedom easily. It is surrendered in response to fear. Most of these defenses we learn as children as a way to handle our fears. These patterns have had years to become entrenched, all the while strengthened by our conviction of their necessity. Patience is needed as it takes time for the defenses to soften in the loving embrace of gentle okay-ness.

Eventually, we discover we can be very naked and very vulnerable while safe and at rest in the silence of the heart. Being with one's fears takes great courage—not to try to change them or fix them, but to be with them in gentle acceptance. A person's fears are individual, growing out of life experience. What takes great courage for one of us to be with may not be problematic for another. We can honor our own courage, hold ourselves in loving non-judgment, and, at the same time, honor the courage of others confronting their own defenses.

Discovering that heartbreak can be an asset is quite transformational. A heart that can be broken can be deeply touched. A heart that can be pierced is a heart that is open to freely receive and send love. The truth we are seeking is ever-present, available in an undefended heart. An open heart allows access to the depth and expanse of the ocean and so deepens our love of Essence that eventually we become one with the Beloved.

The personality can deny the necessity for such openness in order to avoid feeling vulnerable. It can rationalize or intellectualize in an attempt to maintain its defenses. Resistance is nothing but fear in disguise. Courage can be found with awareness of the wave.

We are so afraid of heartbreak, all the while longing to live with abandon. However, recklessness with our hearts is not undefended openness but rather a disguise for our need. We have often given our hearts over to others in hopes that they would give us the love and approval we thought we so desperately needed.

For some, this is a defense in order to avoid loneliness. For others, what they experience as love is heavily flavored with a need to be needed, a bolster for their personality's sense of self-worth. The belief is that if one is needed, one must be of worth. If one can be in control, one will be safer. Such stances attract one to co-dependent relationships, where two people relate primarily from need and want. Truly a setup for suffering!

In order to fill these needs, we may find ourselves once again placing our hearts in the meat grinder of a familiar drama. Ultimately, though, we get tired of cranking the mill and see that what we truly want will not be found in the drama. At this juncture, we can discover an opportunity for more clarity regarding suffering and pain.

Suffering comes from the dramas we create. We fuel suffering with attachments and the plays of the mind. As long as we identify with that which we are not, we will suffer. As long as we collude with our minds and play the "I am not enough" game, we will suffer. There is no way we are not of worth and no need to prove ourselves.

Pain, however, is inevitable in a live body. We will feel pain, but if we don't resist it and let it flow through our bodies, it will move right through. If we gradually live with open, undefended hearts, we will become both more deeply compassionate and susceptible to pain. Our hearts will be pierced by the pain and suffering we see around us, as well as the abundance of love. Our hearts will break and break and break.

Even if we become less defensively reckless, heartbreak will exist. Our heart can be pierced at any moment. Your heart may be as pierced by seeing the deadness in the eyes of the man sitting across from you on a subway as by the unabashed love in the greeting of your beloved dog. Such openness of the heart is being receptive to life in the moment. It is being fully alive.

We cannot control the events of our lives in order to protect our hearts. Such attempts are a drain of energy and will meet with dismay and failure. Difficult events seem to happen, usually unexpectedly. The only control we have is in how we choose to perceive the events. For example, loved ones will die and leave us with a grieving heart, further exposing us to our aloneness. We can choose to be with our grief, letting it engulf us and emerge with a fuller, braver, less defended heart. Or we can remain mired in our grief forever, shut down and deadened.

If we truly let go of the dream propelling any drama, we can embrace a moment of surrender. To release the dream, we need to see it clearly. It may be advantageous to ask ourselves what we would receive if our dream came true. The answer may illumine our desire. Then we have the opportunity to decide if satisfying that particular desire is worth the suffering we are creating.

When we can rest in the silence of the heart, we have discovered the most intimate, enduring friend and are increasingly content with aloneness. The wisdom that comes from the lessons taught by our agenda-fueled ventures enables us to prefer to turn within. As we embrace the ever-flowing love within, we discover we are less captives of our needs and wants. Such a heart is more open and undefended but less prone to defensive recklessness. Instead, we can more readily open our hearts to the full abandon of this endless love.

Eventually, we may surprise ourselves at the open vulnerability we feel in a situation in which we formally would have placed a fortress around our hearts. Family weddings or funerals are often places where we discover archaic defenses emerging, replaying themselves as they did in the past. This time, however, as the family member, whose attacks once caused us to put up a defense, may still behave in familiar fashion, yet our internal and external responses have changed. Comments may even momentarily hurt, but then move right through as we remain rooted in the steady silence. There is no marshalling of our defenses. We remain detached from the comments as there is no longer a need for others' approval or a need for whatever else seemed previously so important.

The lack of suffering on our part is not because we have armored ourselves to be impervious. A new sense of true power emerges in our openness and vulnerability. It is the solidness of knowing who we truly are, who they are, and where true love exists.

At some point in this transformation, we really "get it" that loving ourselves is not only possible, but also essential. Gradually, it becomes easier to fully embrace ourselves, gratefully and often automatically. We become softer, more attuned to the silence within as we surrender our armor. The simplicity of the process is perhaps an unexpected boon. Peace settles as we rest in the deep stillness.

It becomes clear that gently loving ourselves is what enables us to remain in that deep rest. In the process of being gently okay with ourselves, we have allowed a way of being that has fewer and fewer agendas. As we surrender our identi-fications with who we are not, we seek less affirmation from outside to bolster our personalities. Our belief that our minds and personalities know best deteriorates as our trust in the wisdom of the flow increases. Self-love enables us to tolerate being more vulnerable.

One of the most common early fears regarding awakening is the fear that judgment will come our way. Actually, these are our own fears projected onto people in our world. In ultimate reality, this is all a projection. Yet in this relative reality, there are those in our lives who truly will not understand. The numerous people I have spoken to regarding their process of unfolding describe a time when they felt quite separate from even the members of their spiritual community. Their understanding had deepened to a place where they felt simpatico with only a few peers. They had yet to become contentedly immersed in their love affair with Essence. To speak out regarding truth as they now understood it meant experiencing the loneliness of being misunderstood or judged. For those for whom being comfortably alone is a thorny area, this can be a difficult time in their spiritual maturing.

Ultimately we all need to befriend our aloneness. Spiritual unfolding is a solitary undertaking. Great liberation comes from no longer needing another, for indeed there is no other. Each of us may have different areas in which our personalities could well get in the way of our unfolding. For me, befriending my aloneness was the most difficult. We can embrace our aloneness as a gift ticket for liberation, or we can continue to look for the next fix, a new relationship or job, anything to avoid the feeling of loneliness.

There came a time in my personal unfolding when, over a period of four years, many changes took place in my life. Actually, the initial awareness of the desire for change happened soon after my experience of identifying with my perfection. Subsequent to that experience, a deep pull emerged to live my life with increasing integrity, although I am not sure I would have put it in those words at the time.

The first major change was to resign as a faculty member of a psychological institute and soon after to close my private practice. This was a huge shift, as I had identified with being both a trainer and a therapist. Next was a decision to leave the spiritual community with which I had long been affiliated.

The biggest change came when my husband and I mutually decided to end a long-term marriage. The coming apart was not easy, but we took as much care as either of us could muster at any given moment and have maintained a close friendship.

A year after we separated, I got in my car and headed west. I did not know where I was going, just that this was what I was to do. As I traveled up and down the Northwest, I kept returning to one community in Oregon. Living alone now on a farm in the peace and serenity of those mountains was just perfect for me.

Soon after I settled into that community, I felt the pull to go to a video "satsang with Gangaji," yet I avoided doing so for six months. When I finally got beyond my resistance, I knew that this was what I was to do now. While attending my first silent retreat with her, I had the great good fortune to have my first experience of who I truly am. I was ripe for the experience. I live my life in eternal gratitude to Gangaji for pointing me in that direction. Over the next two years, my understanding deepened as did my capacity to *be*. However, I knew that a large part of me was still hanging on, unable to surrender.

Some friends told me they were going to Vancouver to spend four days with John de Ruiter. I felt the pull to go. When I first sat in a room with John, I knew I had been led to what was next in my unfolding. When this awareness surfaced, I remember saying to myself, *Well, are you going to be open and trust this or aren't you?*

When I asked John a question, he did not answer me out loud. Instead, we sat in silence gazing at each other for a long time. Silencing my mind was relatively easy as I resonated with the deep silence that is John, that is us. I went deeper into the nothingness until, suddenly, I dissolved into a whirlpool of endless, incredible love. I have no way to express my enormous gratitude to John but to live my life as consistently as possible in devotion to that little bit of truth that I know. I have discovered that surrender is an ever-deepening, lifelong process.

Many other important teachers came into my world in the form of friends and evolved beings that live ordinary lives in this community. Life itself continues to be the primary teacher. All taught me to deeply trust the flow.

Power and Control

As our eyes clear, apparent is the true identity of those around. Clearly, they are the wave also. Clearly, their unfolding has its own rhythm. Apparent is the arrogance that we have ownership of their lives, that we can or should control them or that we even know best. Less is our need to be in control, to be controlled, or to control others. Less do we need to bolster our security and self-image by controlling others. We may be the guardians of the children in our lives, but we are not in charge of their destiny. The adults in our world also have their own unfolding that we can hold sacred.

A gift of self-love is that we need less the security of feeling we are in control of what happens in our environment. It is readily apparent that who we are cannot be destroyed. The ready-alert defense system can be disarmed. At first, our safety seems a bit shaky in an environment without our defense arsenal. Even though current attacks may still hit their intended target—our personalities—it is reassuring to discover that, since our identities are no longer invested there, neither can we be wounded in the same manner. The relief created by no longer spending our energy maintaining the defense system is palpable.

Another defensive weapon in our armament becomes less potent. That means of defense is projection, a very effective weapon for placing our thoughts and feelings onto others, particularly those we do not want to own ourselves. Projection is an essential ingredient for our minds' creation of stories regarding the thoughts, feelings, and motives of others.

As our security vigilance becomes less active, we care less about others' thoughts or motives and are less prone to invest energy in creating a rationale for others' behavior. As we are increasingly okay with our own thoughts and feelings, we have less of a tendency to project them onto another. We are also less willing to take responsibility for another's feelings and more willing to be responsible for our own. Each of these components reduces projection. This does not mean we do not care about the other. It does mean that we are less invested in protecting ourselves, because we have less attachment to any perceived need for protection.

Our desire is to be in harmony with the wave. Almost unnoticed, needs and wants begin to dissolve. Periodically, we discover we are no longer controlled by a desire for something that previously captured our attention, sapped our energy, and depleted our serenity. In our current resting, the precious moments when only love exists come more frequently. The warmth of love melts the ego, and we become less self-absorbed. What emerges is a new depth and definition of love.

Forgiveness

ALL OF US HAVE HAD EXPERIENCES in our lives in which others did not live up to our expectations: parents who dropped stitches (some parents, numerous stitches), teachers who squelched our creativity, friends who betrayed confidences, or adults who broke important commitments. Some of us have had catastrophic losses at the apparent hands of another.

The resentment and hatred that may be present or stored in our bodies is a heavy burden. Such animosity burdens our bodies, clouds our vision, and affects our vibration. All of us have seen people whose beings were riddled with bitterness and witnessed how it affects their presence. Their vibration has great impact on any gathering. Their lives know little happiness and the chronic tension in their bodies from holding on to the bitterness takes a toll.

To observe the effect of bitterness on another gives us a clue as to what affect a milder version may have on our bodies and lives. To forgive because we do not want to pollute our being with bitterness may not seem particularly noble, yet if we seek to know truth and to live in truth, harboring such anger will deter us.

Holding on to our animosity can serve several functions: one, a defense; another, retribution; and, sometimes, it is a way of avoiding examining one's own behavior in a situation. Somehow, the world seems safer with our guard up. Not only are we defended against whoever was the perpetrator, but we also have a tendency to generalize and condemn as guilty other people we meet with similar characteristics.

If we don't forgive, we will have to remember to maintain our vigil. Such alertness takes great energy. In addition, we keep mistrust alive by feeding it with any indication we see for its importance. All this keeps the past very alive. If we wish to be an ever-purer vehicle for Essence to express itself, our held animosities must go. We are less apt to carry resentments as we become less judgmental with others and ourselves. The true identity of each of us is more continually in our aware-ness. We are open to give and receive unconditional love.

During the almost three decades I was a psychotherapist, the majority of people I saw were adults who had been physi-cally or sexually abused as children. The stories were horrific. The courage they showed to face their fears, unburden their bodies, and open their hearts to loving themselves and others was an inspiration to watch.

Most of them eventually began to talk about forgiveness. Some decided to forgive their perpetrator and walk away to go on with their life, having put their story down. Others decided to forgive, to remain in contact with their abuser, but not to forget. This they felt was necessary for the safety of their own children and other minors in the family. They were able to see their abusers, and those who neglected to protect them, with a more compassionate heart. All felt relief at letting go of the thoughts and feelings that they came to feel were poison to their *being*. They gave me a great lesson regarding forgiveness.

I had some judgments of my own, however. I found it hard to open my heart to abusers. As the flow provided, I was asked to supervise a psychologist who was instituting a program using body-oriented psychotherapy with incarcerated sex offenders. In the program were men who volunteered to participate in extensive psychotherapy. I came to honor the courage of these men as they dealt with the horrors in their own lives.

I was surprised to find, although I should not have been, that most of them uncovered a repressed sexual abuse in their own lives. Many of them had violated a child the same age they were when they were first sexually abused. After dealing with their own abuse, their attraction to children diminished. On a personality level, abuse began to make some sense. Spiritually, what was being played out in the destiny of each of these individuals I have no way of knowing.

One morning, during this time, I woke up with the thought that I had done it all. I really let myself *be* with the possibility that there had been other lifetimes and there was nothing in this human reality that I had not experienced. I could have been an abuser as well as the abused. What amazed me was that it was okay. I could be okay with the possibility that I had once been an abuser myself.

What left me was a whole heap of judgments. I have no way of knowing the validity of these thoughts; it did not matter. The gift was in the acceptance. As I let myself *be* in my heart, it was clear that in absolute reality there is no separate me or you to have done anything. Currently, I have friends who are released sex offenders and who have gone on to be about their own unfolding having never touched a child again. I have a friendship with a man who was convicted for sex offenses he never committed and have learned of the difficulties he and his family faced through his lengthy incarceration.

Perhaps we can't actually walk in someone else's shoes, but we can dare to open our hearts and see them as who they truly are. Perhaps we can even stay in the awareness that whatever happens to them happens to us. That we are separate is only an illusion.

Purity of Love

As OUR LOVE FOR OURSELVES DEEPENS and we identify with who we truly are, we begin to have access to a purer love. This love is never-ending. Filling our beings, it is always available, always fresh and new, yet familiar. When there is a meeting between two people who truly see the other, love is instantaneous. It is the Self meeting itself, loving itself. In those moments, personality is irrelevant. One moves right past the body and the personality into communion with who they truly are.

The love that emanates is a love with open arms, an honoring of the other's unfolding. Gone are the agendas, the need to control, jealousy, envy, and all the plays of the mind and personality that can contaminate love. What remains is a deeper, purer love more beautiful than anything we thought possible. Eventually, one or the other's personality may intrude in such a way as to stomp on the other's toes in a manner that cannot be ignored. Such an intrusion can be respectfully dealt with knowing it is a manifestation of personality on both peoples' part, not a statement of who they truly are.

As we open ourselves to the ever-present wave, love and joy of Essence can permeate every cell of our being, transforming our entire experience of this life. Gradually, we become aware that we are involved in our deepest love affair. That affair is with Essence.

Our hearts are continually singing a love song to our Beloved Essence. This Beloved is the most consistent, steadfast lover we will ever know. Our Beloved is us. We discover that unconditional, pure love is who we are. We are the love beyond words that moved to create the form that holds and sustains us. Such a transformation opens us to see with the eyes of the heart the abundance of love present in the world.

Spiritual Communities

DURING A PERIOD IN MOST PEOPLE'S UNFOLDING, they seek out friendships with others involved in similar spiritual interests. This is particularly true when spirituality moves from being a part of one's life to *being* one's life. We have a tendency to want to share what is important to us. We also enjoy being understood and gravitate toward people with whom we feel we have commonalities. Many of us grew up in families where we marched to the tune of a different drummer and now seek comfort with kindred souls. These needs can strengthen our ties to spiritual groups where we are with others who honor what is most important to us, speak a similar language, support our practices, and help us from feeling alone. This connection may become less important as we unfold, but while the need's presence is felt, participating in spiritual groups has many of the flavors of creating a spiritual family.

Swami Muktananda is reported to have said that, if a group of his devotees were in the same room for long, they would work on each other. Certainly anyone who has lived in a monastery, ashram, or temple for long could testify to the truth of his assertion. Residence in a spiritual community is not essential. Spiritual groups are present in even the smallest of towns. Anyone very active in a church or synagogue may have discovered that the other members both nourish your devotion and push your buttons. Once a button has been pushed, if we meet what emerges with razor sharp honesty and vigilance, we are given gold.

> For a period of years, a meditation group met in my husband's and my home. Members of the group took different responsibilities for the evening's program. We were fortunate to have a large room used only for meditation. The stillness in that room deepened with time, due in part to the accumulative energies of twenty to thirty meditators, who gathered there every Wednesday night. My husband and I had the good fortune to meditate in that space each morning for an hour before we started our day. This group supported each other in their practices and helped each other deepen the understandings of this spiritual tradition. Members became mirrors for each other and were sometimes annoyed with each other. The sign over the arch at the ashram we all attended said "See God in Each Other." That practice became a part of our time together, nourished us, and spilled over into our relationships outside the group.

For some of us, there may come a time when being attached to a particular spiritual community seems too confining, or some of the policies of that community do not seem in harmony with our current understanding. Communities are, after all, made up of divine beings with all their human frailties. Or, we may leave solely because we are responding to an inner pull to spend time with a different teacher or seek solitude. Moving away from a community can be difficult, as one is leaving friends and a way of worshiping or practicing that has been integral to one's life. Often such leaving is met with resistance from friends and partners who want to keep the sanctity of the fellowship they share with us. Some are threatened that our leaving is a statement about the community, its leader, or their own participation.

We can be true, however, to our own inner direction. If we really contemplate our motivations, we will know if our leaving is a copout due to our unwillingness to face a difficult stage in our own unfolding. If that is our reason for leaving, we will most likely take the difficulty with us when we leave. Staying in a community because of fear of leaving and venturing out can be another pitfall that contaminates our clarity. Such a fear can be so loud that it is impossible to hear the guidance to leave calling from within. Once we quiet our fear, we know if we are integrated with our own guidance from deep within and are simply responding to a pull to move on. Whatever our reason for leaving, if not at the time, perhaps in hindsight, our leaving can be without judgment while celebrating what we have been given and cognizant that our unfolding is beautifully orchestrated by our Self.

Tender Kindness

WHEN I WAS REGULARLY ATTENDING THE ASHRAM, one of my favorite times to be there was New Year's Eve. During Swami Chidvalasanda's evening talk, she would give a suggestion of something we might focus on for the coming year. One year, her suggestion was very simple: "Be kind to each other." I took her recommendations seriously, and this became part of my practice. I was surprised how transformative kindness became.

Just to be kind is so simple; all it takes is being in our hearts. We then expand our capacity to see whatever is in the moment through the eyes of the heart. An action may or may not be involved. If one is drawn to act, the action is without an agenda. Gone is seeking to be appreciated or to feel good about ourselves. No longer do we attempt to intervene and fix something. There is just *being* this love.

Even though one is not looking for any return, return comes. Loving brings more joy into our lives. We are *being* the happiness we desire. In addition, love is contagious. Others around us may become more joyful and pleasant to be around. We can create happiness in our lives and bring it into the lives of others. At some point, we discover that kindness no longer needs our attention; it has become a way of life.

Exploring the Golden Treasures

A SIMILAR NOTICING can bring an awareness that gold is to be found in everything that happens in our lives. Seeing this at first may be somewhat more of a stretch as, sometimes, finding the gold in a particular situation is hard. Difficult times come into our lives and the world in general. Seeing the gifts that these situations bring may take hindsight or a totally different perspective. Yet, if we look closely enough, gold is to be found even in what appears to be the direst tragedy. That gold is a treasure for our unfolding.

As I look back over my life, I can see from this vantage the perfection in all the events. Each, no matter how joyous or painful, was an opportunity for unfolding. I stand now in awe of how much grace there has been in the right people showing up in my life at the perfect moment. Some brought great support and help; others, upheaval, but all of it has been a gift. Could I have stayed in the psychotherapy practice, the marriage, and the spiritual community? Some would say I had a choice. If I had let fear be my guide and not listened within, perhaps I could have stayed. But I did not feel like I had a choice if I was to live my life with integrity.

Once we let in honesty and discover the gentle pull of our inner truth, we no longer feel like we have a choice. If we open ourselves so that we can honestly hear the guidance from deep within, we can flow in harmony with Essence. The biggest gift is that we more deeply trust the wisdom of the wave. With that surrender comes a peaceful resting deep within, sustained by a knowing that all is well.

However, our personalities are so powerful that they can twist the concept, "everything happens for the best," and use it in service of the ego. One frequently hears some version of this concept in the New Age spiritual vernacular. Sometimes, this is a rationalization for accepting as divine providence the outcome of some drama one has created and for never truly examining the recurring pattern of behavior. If we look deep enough, we may see the pattern that is creating our struggle. If we dismiss some of the events in our lives as the hand of fate—when actually we have been swimming cross-stream— we may never find the gold that leads us to once again swim in harmony with the flow.

A person came into my office when I was practicing psychotherapy and said he would like to be married, but felt it was not meant to be. He had been married four times and all four wives had left him. Therefore, God was telling him not to be married. There was gold in looking at what he does in relationships that creates so much suffering in his life. His rationale that God was telling him not to marry can be seen as a play of the mind to avoid looking at that gold. Each of us needs to be noticing when we are in surrender, going with the flow, and when we are hypnotizing ourselves with spiritual concepts.

In Service to That Little Bit

PERHAPS EVEN MORE DIFFICULT than seeing the gold in some of the events of our lives is to see the treasures in the events of the larger world. It seems like such a crazy world. We often feel so helpless to have any impact on the chaos. For many, it just doesn't seem enough to be about their own evolution even though it makes sense that this is where it all starts.

As we become cleaner and clearer, so does our way of being in the world. Our vibration changes, and that alteration is felt by others and by the universe. The ripples of our state are endless. Remaining cognizant of the impact of our vibration may be hard for us. Such awareness necessitates remembering that we are all one. Whatever affects one part of the whole affects the totality. Our vibration matters. The energy we put out into the universe matters.

As we live in devotion to that little bit of truth that we know, some people may desire to involve themselves in some cause they feel passionate about. This may be something that involves us in a job or as a volunteer. What is important is not what one does, but one's way of *being* in what one undertakes. If we bring to a situation our righteous indignation as well as contempt for the efforts of others, our vibration negatively affects the situation. However, we impact a situation positively when we come with hearts open to possibilities and inspiring the creativity in others and ourselves. Then we have opened a space for the wave to flow freely.

Our reason for birth is to be about our unfolding. That includes being in truth as we presently understand it, and being this love. That is the way we can be about being in this world. Whatever we do from that space will have a positive impact.

One way devotion expresses itself is in service. When we feel our lives overflowing with abundance and the magnitude of grace that has been bestowed upon us, the tendency is to want to give back. Almost immediately, we realize there is no way we can give in kind. We can, however, *be* an embodiment of that little bit of truth that we know. When we live in harmony with the wave, everything in our lives becomes a cleaner, clearer expression of Essence.

It has long been said that we need to change ourselves first and then attempt to bring about change in the world. This is not a popular statement for several reasons. One is that bringing oneself into harmony with Essence takes time, and in the meantime, it appears that the world desperately needs our involvement. The second is that to be involved in trying to make changes in the world is easier than to be in moment-to-moment honesty with ourselves. Perhaps we can be involved in the causes we are passionate about and remain aware of our way of *being* and the need for noticing with stark honesty. To do so enables us to be in harmony with the wave of Essence. From that awareness, Essence can more freely express itself through our forms.

As we wake up from the dream, we see that this world is an illusion and that there is nothing to do, nothing to fix, and nothing ever really happens. However, as long as we are living our daily lives in this relative reality, we are involved just by being present. Our vibration affects the universe. Our way of being with others and ourselves makes a difference. Many of us have been in the presence of others, who are the embodiment of consciousness in such a way that their inner silence is palpable. The clearness and clarity of their vibration affects the room the moment they enter.

Several former activist friends of mine recently went to a local town board meeting. That evening there promised to be a heated debate over a local issue that had generated passionate feelings. This small group of friends knew they would not submit a petition or probably even speak. They placed themselves throughout the room and just remained open, resting in the flow within. Relatively quickly, the dialog in the room changed from heated negativity to a positive consensus-building dialog.

James Twyman periodically coordinates a peace vigil from particularly troubled spots in the world. People all over the world are notified to pray or meditate at a particular time. Such an event is built on the premise that the collective energies of thousands of people *being* in their hearts affect the vibration of the world. Shortly after a recent vigil, thousands of people marched in peace demonstrations in numerous locations. This also had impact. The vast numbers of people were noticed as well as the way people were *being* in those demonstrations. Had the events become violent, the vibrational impact would have been much different. Making war on war has a different vibrational quality than a peace vigil. The understanding of this vibrational principle is behind Gandhi's process of non-violence, later adopted by Martin Luther King.

I was recently at the home of some friends who have been lifelong activists, as well as spiritual seekers. My host asked my opinion regarding the causes for which he was passionate. My response was that I felt what we did was not as important as how we did it. Our way of being permeates whatever we are about. I could see he was pondering this while others moved the conversation to areas of their concern. After a short time, he looked at me and said that he had been thinking today about the anger and contempt he had for our current President and wondering if, by holding him in this way, he wasn't being as bellicose as the President. Now he was considering my suggestion that it is the manner in which we go about protecting the environment or trying to stop war that is of the greatest importance. Our vibrations affect the world.

I shared with my host that I had stopped reading emails that attempted to motivate peoples' involvement by using fear. To scare people into action is to create a vibration that is counterproductive to the goals they aspire to.

Someone who sends out hundreds of thousands of email messages designed to spread fear not only infects the vibration of anyone whose fear increases, but also changes the individual's own vibration. This person could find the support for causes by speaking to peoples' hearts and the whole tenor of his or her activity would change.

We can become so passionate about a particular cause we have adopted that we become the doer trying to accomplish something or fix somebody. We lose our awareness of the presence of the wave. We diminish our capacity to be a clean, clear vehicle through which Essence can express itself. If we wish Essence to use us, we must surrender control and let the flow express itself through our form.

As we open ourselves more fully, what becomes apparent is that we are consciousness being in each moment. We may be in a body, but there is no longer a difference between inside and outside. What we see around us is consciousness expressing itself in everything. What formally was seen as mundane now has a fascination as a play of consciousness. There is no good or bad. What once seemed evil is now perceived as twisted consciousness finding a way to unravel.

In recent years, much has been written about a vibrational change on the planet. Some have spoken about the quantum impact of increasing numbers of people becoming awake and opening themselves to be clearer expressions of Essence. When enough people's vibrations reach a certain optimum level, the whole vibration of the planet will change. Most of us have experienced how the energy changes in a room of people as they connect deep within. Only a small step is required to imagine a similar impact a larger number of people could have on the vibration of the planet. That time is nearer than many realize.

Going Against the Current

This is your lifetime. It could end at anytime —
Where is your attention?
Where is your prayer?
Where is your song?*

In a fortunate life, comes the call to be free
From the cycle of bondage and misidentity
To wake from the dream and finally realize
The truth of one's being before the body dies
So before the final scene has passed
See the screen on which it's cast
See what's seeing this me and you
And then you will see who
Who you really are

from "Who We Really Are" by Kirtana
* Gangaji's words at a public gathering.

91

Distractions

WE CAN CHOOSE TO SWIM against the flow for as long as we wish, all the while saying that what we truly want is liberation. Essence is abundantly patient; we can take all the time we want and be assured a loving embrace when we return home. We can abandon our awareness of the wave by swimming after some desired "something," all the while using whatever means our personalities and talents can provide to achieve our goals. We can grab a more prestigious job, seduce a friend's husband, or seek political power using dubious means to obtain our trophy. Each is a power game. We are destined to create drama and suffering.

Without our striving, events will happen as they do. To let ourselves rest in knowing that whatever we need will appear takes deep trust and surrender. The job or the partner may appear, and so may an illness or death of someone we love. We have the opportunity to *be* in the flow with these events or create distractions. *Being* with the flow is remaining rooted in the truth, in the awareness that the love we are is always present.

We create distractions when we perceive events with fear—fear that we will not get enough of something our personalities desire, fear that we will not be able to tolerate the pain of the moment. The fears are endless. We lose our footing, forget what we know about the wave, put up our defenses, and go to sleep. In the dream, we don't remember who we are.

Once we take a nap, blaming the distraction by denying any responsibility for our perceptions is easy. The culprit for our predicament becomes our jobs, our relationships, or our lack of money, to name a few of the possible reasons for our suffering. We are unable to see that the way we perceive these events in our lives is the cause of our suffering.

The stronger our connection with the wave, the shorter our nap as our tolerance for the suffering we create is blessedly short. When we awaken from our sleep, we need to be gentle with ourselves. Judgments will put us back to sleep while tenderness is the quickest way to regain our footing and feel the grace of the wave.

Drifting

ANOTHER OPTION IS THAT WE CAN JUST . . . hang out on a raft sunning ourselves, complacent with our current unfolding. To become aware that we are not just resting on the raft, but hanging out there for an extended visit, takes real honesty. The motivation that has caused us to stay on the raft is usually well below the surface of our awareness, not creating any obvious urgency, and can go undetected for some time.

There can be many reasons for spending extended time on the raft. Two of the most common are arrogance and false humility. At first glance, they seem like opposites. Upon closer observation, they appear also to be opposite sides of the same coin. These two characteristics are tricky as their presence can be supported by the personality.

For example, one can take pride in his or her humility, causing the infection of false humility to go undetected for some time. True humility is a deep gratitude for the abundance showered upon one and a knowing that the gifts were freely given, not earned. There is nothing we could ever do to earn the abundance of grace in our lives.

False humility is a sense of not being good enough, a doubting of our worthiness and a forgetting of who we are. False humility is a sense we are not worthy enough for deeper unfolding and see ourselves as less than others. We have been deeply conditioned to make such comparisons, yet such comparisons necessitate we view our unfolding on a linear scale, each of us having our place on the scale while forgetting we are all one.

Arrogance can surface as a pride in what one has attained thus far in his or her spiritual unfolding. This, of course, assumes identification with the personality or the mind as the achiever of our "spiritual behavior" or understanding. Such perception denies who we really are as well as the gifts of grace. Arrogance also shows itself in the perception that what we have achieved is somehow superior to the attainment of those around us.

We can easily get caught up in the game of "who has had the most outstanding experience."

> During lunch with a friend, a beautiful woman who knows who she is, I was sharing my concern regarding putting some of my experiences in this book. I told her one of my concerns was that to do so would be to highlight the peak experiences rather than the moment-to-moment unfolding. Her response was to remind me that I was succumbing to a play of the mind. Friends can hold up such wonderful mirrors.
>
> She said that her realizations were much quieter than mine, yet she knew when her perceptions of reality had changed. She had had quiet transformational experiences. They didn't look like mine, yet they were perfect for her. Some aspects of awareness of the wave seem universal, such as sensing you are becoming more ordinary or realizing how little you know. Other aspects are unique to each of us and, as such, need to be honored for their perfection.

To compare our experiences with those of another can be useful for the purposes of both validating their experiences and realizing the importance of our own. One of the functions of sages and teachers throughout time has been to validate the experiences of their followers. We live in a time when many do not have access to an ongoing communication with a teacher. We can serve that function for each other, particularly those with whom we have intimate heart-to-heart connections.

We can validate and celebrate a transformational experience in the life of another even if it has not been our experience or one that we understand. In a similar manner, we can validate and celebrate the experience of another even when it has taken a form different from our own. It most likely will. Their experiences can provide assurances of the wisdom in opening to truth and venturing into the unknown. Likewise, we can notice when another has become quieter inside or has not been seduced by a familiar drama and honor these transitions. To acknowledge those expressions of deepening both in others and in ourselves is a gift.

Even more insidious is playing the game of "who is the most spiritual among us." In order to play, the personality needs to create a mask. This mask is used to cover any "flaws" that will keep us from winning the game. For example, we might be covering our anger. By the rules of the game, someone who expresses anger is not spiritual, thus losing points. The mask will help us to cover the anger and appear the most spiritual of all. This is a deadly game, one our Puritan forefathers were quite good at.

A version of the game was played by most of us as children by putting on a mask of the good boy or girl in order to win love. The price of winning the game was very high—we buried aspects of our personalities and put on personas. Most of us spent many adult years discovering the many faces of these masks and attempting to discard them forever.

To put on a mask of "spirituality" is just another version of the same game, equally as deadly or perhaps even more. Again, we are using a familiar game to cut ourselves off from the awareness of the love we truly are. As long as we wear masks and don personas, we place blocks in the way of easy access to our innermost being. Winning the "spiritual game" may or may not win us applause from some peers. We already know the warmth of that accolade fades fast. The big loss in wearing the mask and playing the game is to loosen our connection with who we truly are.

Not only can others be validating, but they can also expose whatever vestiges remain of our latent tendencies to play spiritual games. Once exposed, these remnants can be dissolved in the arms of gentle okay-ness. If, however, we find ourselves sharing with another person who consistently avoids honestly looking at his or her own tendency to play the games, such as, "I have a deeper understanding than you," it may be time to share with someone else. This change can be made without judgment, respectfully honoring what nourishes our own unfolding.

Hanging out on the raft is certainly seductive. We lull ourselves into thinking we have forever, not wanting to face the prospect that our lives could end at any moment. Huge hunks of our lifetimes can be spent lounging and basking, complacent with our current understanding. Perhaps we have established residence on the raft because we have inklings that, if we jump back into the water, there will be a whirlpool downstream we won't want to swim through. If we surrender while in a whirlpool, it will take us to the deep and spit us back out.

While napping on the raft, we are not opening ourselves to fulfill our true desire. Ultimately, truth is the only thing that can fulfill our longing. Hopefully, we will venture into our vulnerability and discover a new definition of courage. The paradox of true power is in vulnerability.

A friend said to me that he thought of himself as a very spiritual person. However, he did not want to become more spiritual as he thought his life would become boring. His image was not that he would get pulled into a cloistered life or that he would adopt a strict moral code of behavior. It was that he would become more like those folks he observed connected with various spiritual groups.

The lives of these people appeared no longer to include many of the activities he most enjoyed. For him, happiness was connected with doing things he enjoyed, and he was not yet able to comprehend any other way to bring pleasure into his life. He was not willing to give up these known pleasures.

He is not unique. Many of us have seen individuals we perceive as more evolved than ourselves and have noted they no longer seem to involve themselves with something we could not imagine our lives without.

There is some truth in my friend's observation. As we mature spiritually, what we are attracted to gradually changes. As our hearts become more open and our bodies less defended, we become more vulnerable. The environments in which we are comfortable change.

We may find ourselves drawn to less violent movies or listen to softer music. Our love affair with ourselves deepens. We are more comfortable being alone and less inclined to fill our lives with activities that we no longer enjoy. Solitude becomes a way of enjoying ourselves. Nature becomes our companion. A long walk in the woods with a dog becomes as pleasant as a long chat with an intimate friend. The awe and wonder of a flower or the feeling of a grandchild's hand in ours can pierce our hearts.

Life becomes an increasingly deeper affair of the heart. We can trust that our evolution will take place. All we need do is listen to our innermost truth and choose in each moment to respond to that truth or not. Our response depends on where our attention is, where our devotion is placed. We can live in devotion to the things we pursue and hope we find what we are looking for. Or, we might better live in devotion to that truth that we know and live our lives in a moment-to-moment reflection of that truth.

Whatever we have used as a deterrent ultimately does not give us what our hearts long for. Eventually, we stop suffering and struggling against the current and go with the flow. When we are truly honest with ourselves, we see that we created our diversions in order to avoid our fear of something. Telling the truth will bring that something to light. Using the sword of honesty to slice through our self-deception takes courage. All we need is available to us in the wave. Once we illuminate fear, we can *be* with it, hold it in love, until it subsides to be replaced by trust and surrender to the flow.

Flowing in Relationships

As I fall into this embrace
I feel your arms extending into space
While a love that will not rest
Blows through my open chest

And tears fall from my heart like rain
Like liquid love pouring from the slain
Glistening with grace.
Christening my face

from "This Embrace" by Kirtana

Being in Relationship

Two people who encounter each other and really see the other
have created what John de Ruiter calls a "bond of being." This
is a connection not based on attraction to the other's body or
compatibility of personalities, but recognition of Essence in
the form of the other. Such encounters may be fleeting or
lifelong. We can have such a connection with a child we meet
or with the person checking out our groceries. That moment is
one of pure seeing, and then one moves on. The same bond
of being can be the fabric of our relationships with those who
regularly inhabit our lives.

A solid bond between two people who have open, soft-
ened hearts is a union of pure intimacy. When we establish
this kind of a bond with another, we still come to know each
other's personalities well. Certain character traits amuse and
delight us while others are difficult. But, in such a bond, as
much as we recognize the loved one's personality, we most
often move right past traits and connect with Essence. In a
similar manner, we recognize the form of that loved one, but
also know their body is not who they are. This is a relationship
with no script as to how it should be. Each person has established their firm connection with their Beloved within and,
therefore, has few if any needs or wants their partner is
expected to meet.

Many of the experiences that contribute or detract in the
process of unfolding come from sharing our lives with those
with whom we have intimate relationships—our partners, our
children, and our closest friends. Maintaining the constancy of
this true bond of being within our more permanent relationships is nectar in life. These relationships provide an ongoing

environment for us to *be* the purity of love that we are. They are a gift for us to express our love and to share our lives with another person who is a reflection of our true selves. Indeed, our own selves!

Inherent in these close relationships is the opportunity to expose those aspects of our minds and personalities' conditioning that pollute the purity of our love and create suffering. All that is needed is an openness to see, the sword of honesty and gentle okay-ness with the other and ourselves. In these intimate relationships can be ones in which both people are committed to their own and the other's unfolding. Both perceive this relationship as a nurturing place to be in truth and to support each other to that end.

Couples can create spiritual partnerships. Friends can create spiritual partnerships. A spiritual partnership is a commitment between two people to be a mirror for each other, to gently awaken each other to their true identity when they have taken a nap. Each supports the other's self-inquiry rather than providing a prescription for how the other should be. Spiritual partners have an agreement to suggest a partner take notice when they are heading cross-current toward a familiar distraction. However, this does not mean trying to "fix" the other.

Likewise, there is a commitment to acknowledge and validate each other's unfolding. Also present is an openness to let each other *be* their own individual expression of Essence. Spiritual partners can see the divinity in one another and remind each other of their okay-ness. This partnership is based less on similar beliefs and concepts than it is on a way of *being* with each other that rings true in the core. Absent is the need to convert the other to one's current understanding.

The community in which I live has several small groups of approximately four people each, who have spiritual partnerships. A deep intimacy and trust has been developed as they have created a non-judgmental environment where they honor each other's unfolding. These groups use as their focus, *The Work*, a model for inquiry developed by Byron Katie and put forth in her book, *Loving What Is*.[1] She suggests four useful questions for enabling us to see more clearly how our beliefs create suffering and how we can let go of the painful thoughts and return to reality. For some people, using such a model can be a helpful structure for spiritual partnerships to *be* together and assist each other.

Partnerships

LET'S DEFINE PARTNERSHIP as any two adults involved in a coupled relationship. These relationships initially become established because of a physical attraction, an emotional attraction, or some kind of spiritual harmony, frequently in that order.

Physical attraction to another creates many sensations in our bodies, a rush that often expresses itself in arousal. Such an attraction is basically sexual; it is nature's way of bringing two sexual people together. Usually, most any relationship based on physical attraction burns itself out within a relatively short time. Yet, sex is the most frequently used criteria for people coming together, even those looking for a more enduring relationship. Many of us are aware that we are attracted to a certain body type or physical attribute. We may have repeatedly ventured into relationships based on this attraction only to have discovered one more time that it is not enough.

As we mature, we are more apt to be drawn to an individual because of aspects of their personality. We may be drawn to those whose character traits we find compatible.

Some seek out a partner they are physically attracted to along with their second criterion, personality traits. Others dismiss the physical and are attracted to an emotional bond with another's personality. The resulting relationships may indeed be sexually fulfilling with much energy spent on working on the relationship through the personality mix.

Some people may be primarily interested in the physical and emotional attraction between them; however, they may decide to limit the pool of perspective partners to those of their particular religious group. This may or may not bring a spiritual dimension to the relationship.

Most of us have entered into relationships based on physical attraction or compatibility of interests and personalities. These relations can deepen and develop into relationships that are bonds of true being.

What is missing in both the physically and emotionally based relationships is that no one is seen for whom one truly is. One has established a love relationship based on that which changes, not what is eternally constant. The body becomes older, and emotional compatibility wanes as people grow and change.

The lack of a deep, spiritual connection with a partner may not be significantly felt until we begin to increase our awareness of being in the wave. At that juncture, we may wish to share with our partner what has become the center of our lives. What becomes primary is not the physical attraction or the emotional compatibility but a deep spiritual harmony. This bond of being emanates from two people truly recognizing the other.

The depth of connection can be confusing to some people who are used to such intensity being sexual. Two people may have a heart-to-heart connection, honoring the Essence in the other, fully aware of the other's gender and sexuality, but not have a bond that expresses itself sexually.

In a bond of being that is a sexual relationship, the love affair that develops is with each other's form and Essence, all in one. Two people enjoy each other's bodies while involved in a much deeper communion, a lovemaking with Essence. Sexuality is a powerful force and such a union needs a container provided by two people *being* with each other. People wishing to express their sexuality through *being* together do not usually move into a sexual union until they have established such a container. A sexual relationship such as this can become a powerful aspect of each person's unfolding, as well as an opportunity to experience great pleasure, ever expanding and deepening one's capacity to both feel and express love. Sexuality can be a celebration of Essence as well as a shared oneness.

In partnerships committed to supporting each other's unfolding, both people desire to live their lives in as much truth and integrity as each is capable of at any given moment. Also present is the realization that each person's process of unfolding is unique to him or herself, and there is no desire to control the other. To do so would be to interfere with the other's flow with the wave.

A fear often expressed among those evolving spiritually is that they could end up celibate. That is a decision some people make. Others decide to *be* celibate for a period of time. One does not usually feel the pull to venture into celibacy until one knows how to access the continual sustenance of love from within. So many of our sexual encounters are a search for love. If one feels that love from inside, one has less need to seek it on the outside. Most of us do need intimacy in our lives, and many who have spoken to me regarding being celibate have close, intimate, non-sexual friendships.

If one enters a period of celibacy, the degree to which sex has previously run one's life becomes readily apparent. With this awareness may come an aversion to any desire having a strong hold. Certainly common is a diminished desire to involve oneself in the sexual conquest game. The recognition of how one can easily slip into agenda-based behaviors, as well as diminished comfort in these encounters, becomes clearer.

To seduce an acquaintance may provide physical release and an ego boost but not create the depth of union that comes from a strong bond of being. For some, casual encounters lose their appeal, especially if they have come to know the possibility of a deeper sexual union.

Sex is a powerful force that can be very consuming. Most all of us have wounds and hurts in our sexual history that we have consciously or unconsciously been attempting to heal. For many, self-destructive behaviors have been deeply entrenched. One needs to be tender with oneself if one chooses to experience celibacy, as it may raise to the surface many buried unresolved issues. Held in the warmth of gentle okayness, these old issues can dissolve.

Some people make the decision to remain celibate. I know of adults, both married and single, who have made that choice. Others remain open to *being* sexual but will no longer tolerate sex running their lives. Celibacy is not the only way to bring clarity to one's sexual life. Noticing habitual or agenda-based behaviors that diminish the clarity of one's sexual expression is possible and perhaps enough for most people to bring liberation to their sexuality.

Change in Relationships

As spirituality becomes the primary interest in our lives, others with whom we have intimate relationships are affected. Fortunate are the partners who share a common commitment to truth. Often, however, one member of a couple becomes involved in a spiritual search while the other partner does not.

A similar situation can exist in our relationships to those within our extended families.

Respecting these differences becomes the curriculum. Exposing loved ones to that which has become important to us may or may not feel appropriate. Sometimes, just telling them about our experiences is enough. Other times, keeping our truth alive in their presence is the strongest and most appropriate statement. Attempts at conversion most usually meet with resistance. The objects of our evangelical efforts will probably not feel respected or honored in their own rhythm of unfolding. Perhaps there is no desire to become involved at the present time and that is their organic response. We can remind ourselves that everything unfolds in its own rhythm. All is well!

Perhaps our motivation for conversion is founded on the need for them to be in communion with our unfolding. Such communion is impossible, since even the most simpatico partner will have their own developing capacity for openness, honesty, and the ability to love themselves. Attempts on our part to feel we know what understanding they should have or how they should go about being "spiritual" are wonderful mirrors for us to see our own personalities' tendency for power and control. Such intrusiveness is quite different from being a spiritual partner. Where control or conversion create havoc between two people, resulting in a marked discordance in vibration, it may be difficult to create a significant enough bond of *being* for a spiritual partnership to be nourishing for both parties.

One thing is certain: relationships change. Relationships need breath and nourishment to grow and change. If we open our arms and our hearts for others to be their true selves, the resulting relationship will not be something we have molded. For if we try to mold another into being something that we want them to be, it is only their personality that is affected.

We can try to change another's personality, but, usually, we fail dismally. To look within ourselves is much more successful. Keep in mind, however, that who each of us truly is will never change.

Partners obviously have their own unique set of distractions. We can become mirrors for each other and, to the best of our ability, provide an environment of gentle okay-ness. This may be easy to do until we simultaneously bang into each other's distractions, and both lose awareness of the wave.

Such a collision is fertile ground for the creation of a drama. Discovering how to be present yet detached, unwilling to be a performer in a loved one's drama, is important. We feel pulled to play a familiar role. As soon as we can bring to our awareness that we have been snagged or are about to be snagged into a familiar role, we are in that moment more able to reconnect with the silence within and reestablish our awareness of being in the wave.

Another pitfall is to try to help our partners with the hope of changing them. For those of us who have identified ourselves as helpers, the transition out of the role of fixer may be difficult. The helper is a highly seductive role. Often there is a denial of the use of helpfulness as a way of maintaining control. Helpers generally have big hearts and receive tremendous pleasure from loving. They may have learned as a child that the way to get love was to give it, or they may have equated loving with doing. "How can I stand here and see you in discomfort and not do something" may be their inner stance.

Much has been written, particularly in regards to addiction, that our need for helping enables the drama of addiction to continue. We may want to gradually shed our identification with being the helper both for ourselves and for those with whom we have a relationship. We might better devote our energy to going within and expanding our capacity to be open and vulnerable. Then, we can discover that to be present in our hearts with compassion is an even more effective way to be with another.

Hoping to sustain a relationship, we commonly give up too much of ourselves. The tendency to listen solely to another while neglecting our own inner wisdom, or to make unwanted compromises in order to have peace, can create difficulty in partnerships. The resulting consequence hinders our own unfolding.

The deepest reason for the relationship may be to butt us right up against our own issues of living from our truth as opposed to compromising for reasons connected to identification and attachment. Perhaps we may even have come to grips with our fears of being alone. When we can come from our deepest selves, we can come to another person in openness and discover ways either to live in honesty with that person or find the courage to move on alone. We cannot change another or force them to live our truth.

As our capacity to love both others and ourselves becomes more unconditional, love becomes cleaner and clearer. The tendency to do something in order to get something diminishes. As we fill our cups with self-love, we are less desperate to drink from outside ourselves. There is less of a need to give love in order to get it in return or to have control over the situation.

Our hearts are so full of the love from within that external love, while felt and appreciated, is less and less needed to maintain our sense of well-being. As our propensity to mold or fix another diminishes, we can appreciate who they truly are and let them *be* while offering support when it is welcomed. Ultimately we know that any personality change or letting loose of attachments and identifications must come from within. As our love for others and ourselves becomes increasingly unconditional, our relationships become easier.

Two people may have decided to be in relationship, but that does not mean that their unfolding will be in harmony. Each one of us unfolds in our own rhythm. Many of the awakened people I know have had several marriages or many relationships. On the surface, relationships may appear to have broken-up for a variety of reasons. For some couples, the rhythm of their unfolding seems too disparate. Perhaps one is gravitating to a quieter, less cluttered life, and the other is maintaining a pretty hectic pace while striving to get and achieve in the world. As their lives appear to be headed in different directions, they no longer seem to share in common what is most important to each of them as individuals.

Others may repeatedly recreate a similar situation. Perhaps they perpetually place themselves in relationship with a partner who perceives life as an on-going drama. When they no longer need to play the role of the rescuer in the drama, the dynamics of the relationship have been profoundly altered. Each time we "get it" that we are doing the same thing one more time and hold this pattern in awareness and gentle okay-ness, the pattern has an opportunity to dissolve, and we have released another particle of clutter from our bodies and personalities. Such a release makes way for more of the radiance from deep within to move closer to the surface.

One of my awakened friends recently told me she had been married four times. She gently laughed at herself as she said, "I kept marrying the same man. When I finally got it and stopped, the pattern was finished." She is not unique. Many have repeatedly experienced being in relationships with others, who all eventually display similar traits, yet they were sure that *this* time they had found a partner without "the problem." People who repeatedly involve themselves with an individual who has an addiction to alcohol often illustrate this. Transformation has taken place when we realize the habit of our patterns and stop them by reminding ourselves with some version of "been there, done that, not doing it anymore."

Relationships change, and the form of relationships may also change. Going separate ways can feel like a great tearing apart. In order to create distance, many couples fall into blaming and faultfinding, both in themselves as well as the other. Blame and fault are concepts of the mind. Coming apart is not without heartache, yet it can be accomplished by being gently okay with our partners and ourselves. Such a transition is a stark opportunity to *be* the truth that we know. Love can change form and means of expression; it does not have to be destroyed.

Great integrity is needed in order to be so honest with ourselves that we know when we are running away from a relationship or, equally problematic, when we are frozen in place by an inner fear of moving on. When we run, we are letting fear make the decision. In staying, even while hearing the voice from within to move on, we are also letting fear make the decision. Truth takes the courage to be honest enough with ourselves that the fear can be exposed. Once exposed, fear can be held in the warmth of our gentle acceptance of its existence. Fear will dissolve and possibly reappear, but when it does, it can be greeted again by acceptance. Denying the existence of our fears only gives them the power to run our lives.

Being with Children

CHILDREN COME INTO OUR LIVES as a trust for our care and nurturing. *Being* with children delights and humbles us. I have never met anyone who has felt they were as good at parenting or teaching as they would like to be. Much has been written on these subjects. Here I wish only to comment on the spiritual unfolding of the children who bless our lives.

Numerous people have shared with me a spiritual event in their childhood that, as a child, they knew better than to tell the adults in their world. At a young age, they recognized that their experiences would not be honored or appreciated, so they buried them, keeping them safe as internal treasures, not sharing them with anyone until they reached adulthood.

One man told me about being on the playground as a boy and seeing this being floating on a cloud just above his head. Years later, he met this same being whom he recognized instantly. The man became his spiritual teacher. We live in a culture that is skeptical regarding such experiences, and children learn this very quickly.

There are presently on the planet many children who are very evolved, many of them possessing a deeper understanding than the adults in the world around them. For me, labeling them as special kids seems unfortunate; they are not unique. As I have said before, there is nothing unique about where anyone is in their understanding. To label these kids as such sets them apart in a way that may or may not be useful to them. It takes sensitivity, however, on the part of the adults in their world to be guardians of their unfolding without being intrusive. As children, they need us to create structure for them, and they need to feel our support. They also have much to teach us if we can remain open to their wisdom.

Recently a mother told me about a "God talk" she had had that morning with her four-year-old daughter, who had said, "I know that, when I die, I get to come back as a baby." Although reincarnation was not necessarily a part of the belief system of the Roman Catholic mom, she had the wisdom to reply, "You know, you just might be right." Her daughter's response was, "I know I am."

The mother had left a channel open for communication with her daughter. She also left open within herself the possibility that her four-year-old might just be right. Can we be open to be taught by our children about the most important questions in our lives? What they tell us may challenge our beliefs. In addition, some of these kids have well-developed "bullshit" detectors. They know when we are being less than honest with them and ourselves. For them to be in our lives is a great gift for keeping us honest and present on the wave.

One day, a thirteen-year-old boy came to my office for his weekly visit. We had been seeing each other for about six months. I was his most recent in a long line of psychotherapists. On this day, he gave me a look I had come to recognize in someone wondering if he or she dared trust me with something important.

As we played checkers, he told me he heard sounds all the time. I did not think he was having auditory hallucinations, so I suggested we listen together as we played. Every now and then I asked him what just happened, and he would tell me.

Eventually, he looked startled and said, "You hear it too!"

I replied, "Yes, what you are hearing is the sound of the universe. Some people's ears can pick it up and some can't. You are one of the lucky ones."

He looked puzzled and asked, "Has anyone ever called you psychotic?"

I laughed and told him no, actually, nobody ever had, and he wasn't psychotic either. "But I hear it all the time!" he replied.

I said that, as far as I knew, he would hear it for the rest of his life. He left my office that day very relieved. We can honor these children, support and nourish them, and allow the possibility that they have many gifts to give us. Or, we can attempt to mold them, suppress them, and diagnose them as pathological. If we do that, however, everyone loses.

No Other

NOTHING EXISTS BUT US; we are everything seen and unseen. There is nothing personal—no me, no mine. Every relationship is a relationship with our own self. The implications of really *being* a manifestation of this understanding are alarming to anyone's sense of personal self. To live one's life as an expression of non-duality erodes a sense of boundaries and dissolves the concept of a separate self and separate other.

To hear people verbalize their current concept of oneness is not unusual. We are all one. We are all divine. We are consciousness. For many of us, all these statements resonate as truth. We can even have an experience of self-realization and more deeply come to understand the truth of these statements. Yet, to *be* the truth of this understanding is challenging—so challenging that many balk, perhaps blocking any further unfolding.

The prospect of there being only me and no other can be a total threat to the sense of one's personal self and one's personal relationships. One can deeply inquire into the question, Who am I? without uncovering the related questions, Who are you? and What are relationships? The threat to a sense of personal self can be so great that, unfortunately, the investigation does not continue any further.

In absolute reality, there is no personal me, no personal you, and no such thing as a personal relationship. In this relative reality, everything appears to have taken separate form and is in relationship with other forms. Being in a body, however, does not change the truth of who we are and what constitutes everything we see before us, including the other human forms with whom we find ourselves in relationship. We are all one. Each of us is the totality. We certainly appear to vary in appearance, in personality, in understanding, but not in what constitutes who we really are.

In a similar fashion, we come to understand the divine in others. Initially we see the light in their eyes and feel their radiance. Certainly, we understand that they are not their ideas or concepts. We may be attracted to their body, but we are aware there is more to them than a body. When we really look into their eyes and see, we know there is more to them than their personality. We may be aware that what is reflected in those eyes is Essence, and that this Essence is the truth of who they are and the truth of who we are, and there is no separate them and us.

As we are aware of the wave, we increasingly connect with friends and acquaintances heart-to-heart, resonating with their Essence. Instant intimacy is created when one is present in an Essence-to-Essence heart encounter. Such intimacy and vulnerability happens when both people allow the nakedness of the encounter. Initially, we may hide from such openness, but gradually our tolerance for being naked and vulnerable expands. Eventually, we find ourselves able to remain un-guarded with whomever we are in contact. There is no "me" to be protected. The Essence in the other person is in the foreground of our attention; their appearance, traits, and patterns remain in the background.

When we truly begin to integrate *no me, no mine,* and *no other,* we fuel the fire that is burning our attachments. If no real boundary exists between an illusory me and an illusory you, then relationship is also illusory. Each of us has a person-ality that wants to feel seen, listened to, understood, and loved. No one exists to meet the needs and wants of a *me.* There is no me to be personally affronted or other to be affronted by. Actually, no other to make love to. We may enjoy the pleasure of a person's body, but we are making love to ourselves in celebration of Essence. Ultimately, we come to see ourselves, listen to ourselves, understand ourselves, love ourselves, and everything is ourselves.

There is great resistance to these implications as it is not how our personalities want it to be, as if wanting it to be different would change things. However, we can choose to not be open to the possibilities and remain only in the world of relative reality. We can choose to perpetuate the illusion that we have control, that this separate self is the doer, that there is another out there, our soul mate, who will complete us, make us whole. We can continue our quest to satisfy our desires and invest our energies in whatever illusions, needs, or wants are generated in the moment. We already know that the satisfaction of fulfilling these desires will be only momentary. Or we can gently let our illusions dissolve and rest in unity. To truly *be* a non-individual in this relative reality necessitates contemplating one's sense of aloneness and how one is in relationship to others.

Alone, Loneliness, and Solitude

To MAKE PEACE with one's sense of aloneness is abundantly liberating. Awakening is a solitary affair of the heart. In this relative reality, we all ultimately make this journey we call a life by ourselves. We stand by ourselves in our own truth. We are in the wave of creation. From that wave, a light emerges to shine through this radiant body we call ours.

In this form, we have a sense of separateness. While we believe we are separate, we are prone to long for another and to be lonely when that other isn't there. In our separateness, we can sometimes feel that we are outside looking in on what we perceive others' have and we think we want. Often when we feel excluded in some way, we are telling ourselves a story that we are "not enough," and this is the reason for our being left out. This fantasy is not only our imagination, but it solidifies and deepens our loneliness. If we perceive we need to relate to another body or personality in order to be whole, to not be lonely, we are doomed to be disappointed. No other can provide our happiness. Happiness and an endless source of love can be found within. All the love we need to nourish ourselves and give to others can be found inside ourselves in endless abundance.

If we are single, we may want a relationship. We might have even created a romantic fantasy that "out there somewhere" is our soul mate. When we find him or her, we will find happiness. And then there are those in difficult relationships who may long to be single again. Usually the desire to be single again is coupled with the hope that we can find another who will finally make us happy.

The need for another to complete us places a heavy burden on any relationship. Disappointment is inevitable as long as we maintain the dream that our prince or princess is "out there." All we need do is find them and we will be happy. No one can give us our happiness. As long as we continue to look for it outside ourselves, we rob ourselves of the opportunity to explore and *be* with the richness of love within. Maturity and the capacity for purity of love come from such an exploration.

As our unfolding progresses, most of us seem to seek out more and more solitude and time away from the distractions of our hectic lives. At first, these retreats seem precious. Eventually, we find them essential. A regular dose of solitude that was once a means of simply replenishing ourselves moves into a means of maintaining awareness of the wave. Somewhere in the process of becoming gentler with ourselves, we discover that we are our own best company. Awareness of the wave reminds us that solitude is essential to our unfolding. During a solo walk in the woods, we feel the rhythm of nature and more keenly sense our internal silence. The silence within beckons us to its presence more and more frequently. Slowly, we become aware that the internal silence graces us with its continual presence whether we are alone or in a crowd.

For those of us who have previously found our nourishment and affirmation in relationships, this turning within can be a difficult and courageous process. Fabricating distractions is easier than finding and resting in the comfort of our aloneness. We may not be aware that we are avoiding aloneness or that we fear being alone will lead to loneliness. Venturing into yet another relationship, taking on a more demanding job, or succumbing to any number of demands on our time is more familiar, seems more exciting. Actually, what we are doing is running from our fear of being alone. At its worst, we clutter our lives, fill them with activities, and even "fall in love" because we cannot be alone. We bring to this love relationship the burden of our need, along with a high probability of becoming unhealthily enmeshed as we hold tightly onto the other in order to keep from facing our aloneness. The result-ant relationship becomes something other than that which we had hoped.

In a deeper, truer sense, all longing is a longing to go home, a yearning to go deep into silence until we become one with the silence of the universe, merging with nothingness and traveling deep into the swirling pool of love from which we came. We can be one with Essence while living in this reality. Once surfaced, that longing, that urge, will not be ignored. A new job, a new relationship, or fulfilling any other perceived desire will not suffice. The pull to be home is stronger and more persistent than any desire we can create. How exquisite that we are complete within ourselves. Everything that we

could possibly need or want is inside ourselves. All the love
we could ever want is deep within and increasingly available as
we become more aware of being the wave. We discover that
we *are* endless love.

A Deeper and Deeper Surrender

Trust me
Trust the beingness you are
I breathed you here
I've carried you this far

And open to whatever is and see
Whatever is
Is always only me

Not in imagined futures
Or in remembered pasts
But only here, and only now
Will you find a peace that lasts

from "Meet Me" by Kirtana

Surrendering to Ourselves

WE LIVE IN THESE BODIES in this relative reality, blessed with a human lifetime. The wave has held us and sustained us even when we have not been aware of its presence. At times, we have flowed with the wave, opening to and absorbing truth. These times are not always easy. No one has promised otherwise. At times, the current seems to be taking us in a direction our personalities do not wish to go. We can go with the flow or change our course. If we decide to go against the flow, we will sense discordance. Something just doesn't feel right. If we stop for a moment and really listen to our Self, we find our way back into harmony with the flow.

Other times, we swim against the flow, unconscious of our detour because we are intent on fulfilling some need or want. Our desires may find momentary pleasure, but eventually, if that pleasure remains based on need and want, we will create a drama. Some of the dramas begin to feel all too familiar. We need to celebrate that realization; it may be the messenger needed to return to awareness of the flow. Finding ourselves again in harmony with the flow may only require removing our attention from our minds and placing it in the silence of our hearts. There, we may discover a physical sensation, a warmth in the heart, a recognizing that our heart is singing. Increasingly, we are in harmony with the wave. Distractions become less frequent and shorter lived. Once noticed, returning to awareness of the wave becomes instantaneous.

Devotion

DEVOTION IS THE ONLY ATTACHMENT WE NEED, the attachment to truth. Devotion is *being* that little bit of truth that we know, living our life in an increasingly consistent fidelity to that truth. Each time we remember the wave, each time we listen to our hearts sing and be with the ever-deepening silence within, we are *being* in devotion. Each time we remember who we are and stop ourselves from falling asleep and dreaming we are our stories or "somebody," who is justified in feeling offended by "another's" act, we are *being* devotion. Each time we honor truth over self-deception, loving acceptance over self-depre- cation, simple acts of kindness over self-absorption, we are *being* in devotion. Each time we see a familiar distraction and stop ourselves from participating by a reminder of "been there, done that, don't need to do that any more," we are *being* in devotion.

What we give our attention to is what we are devoted to. In the past, we lived in devotion to certain dramas, suffering, beliefs, and desires that consumed our lives. As we commit ourselves to truth, we can gradually see that we are no longer participating in many familiar dramas, giving us blessed relief from the reruns. Every time we have honestly discovered truth by examining our beliefs and patterns, we have loosened the way in which consciousness has twisted itself to accommo- date our thoughts. Truth unravels consciousness in our surface bodies, resulting in a free, undistorted flow. Access to the core of our being and the wave of Essence becomes unblocked, allowing us to be in harmony, softer, more recep- tive, trusting that the flow will take us where we are to go and use us in whatever way it wishes. We become ever more radiant as the light from within has access to shine through our form. We get to be in the joyful flow, our hearts singing in gratitude and reverence at the indescribable magnificence of it all.

I have heard self-realized acquaintances state that every breath they take is in devotion. For me, that would be a pretty pretentious statement to make at this point. There is a personality that still exists and a mind that I still catch myself abiding in for brief times. What is clear to me is that devotion, like surrender, is an ever-richer, ever-deepening love affair with myself—for my Self is Essence.

No Preference

ONE OF THE FEW THINGS on which we can rest assured is the fact that everything changes, that is, except what never changes—who we truly are. We are abundantly blessed that we can come to rest in the tender happiness of that which never changes. From the endless stillness of home, we can observe this movie we call life. The scenes will come and go, as will the characters. The storyline will have constant changes and predictable recurring themes. Feelings will envelop us; some will pierce our hearts. As thoughts come, they are observed, then quickly pass through the mind. Their companions, opinions and judgments, become less frequent visitors and are seen but not take seriously.

We find interest in parts of the story, amusement with others, for we humans are a humorous lot. As our surrender deepens, much of the story just flits by. We are in this world but detached; however, we are not indifferent. Our home is a space of deep compassion for the suffering of others, yet there is no need to move in and take charge or fix anything. We are content at home with no need to be the designated helper and without want for anything.

At some point, we are bound to ask ourselves, *Who is it that is writing the story of this movie I call my life?* There really is only one answer and that is—we are. There is no other to be the writer. We are that! We are the writer, the projector of the movie, as well as the characters on the screen.

Events don't just happen to us. Nobody is doing anything to us. Some would say that we energetically draw to ourselves that which we need. Others would state a similar assertion but call it intention, and still others would call it karma.

What is clear is that we have a choice as to how we perceive the events of our lives. We can either choose to see whatever is happening as something that is happening *to* us, or we can see it as an opportunity provided for our unfolding. We have a choice to cut through the surface to core honesty and be with the truth of any situation. Anything that happens in our lives can either be perceived and experienced as a support for our unfolding or an adhesive that enables us to remain stuck. If we are aware of being the wave and surrender to the flow, life will take care of itself.

At one point in my life, I was actively involved in conscious intention. One question that kept haunting me was, what was the interplay between conscious intention and surrender? I still do not know the answer. My conscious intentions were always for the highest good of all. Yet, stating such intentions seemed to have conceptual underpinnings that my mind knew best what was needed. Finally, I came down on the side of surrender. My mind and personality cannot write a script that could possibly be an improvement on what the wave of Essence provides.

In addition, there was uneasiness with the question of who is the doer? We can intend something, and it may happen. Seeing our personalities as the doer will only be a diversion from our moment-to-moment awareness of who we are and the endless love present with that realization. Our minds and personalities are not the doer, Essence is. Everything that has happened in my life has happened for the best. What had emerged with this realization is a resting, a peace in the deep trust that all is well.

From the space of surrender, there is no longer any preference, no desire that anything happen a certain way— just a deep knowing that everything happens for the best. Life can be experienced as living in two worlds. We live in this reality and in these bodies as we are expanding our awareness of absolute reality. A time then comes in our evolution where we may feel a bit split, as if we are living in two different worlds. However, as we become more comfortable in each reality, we lose preference over which reality we are experiencing and are complete in the moment.

The wave may bring any variety of events into our lives. Whatever it is doesn't matter. As long as one remains in that awareness, there is no dread of the future, no anxiety about what might happen next, just a deep trust that what happens will happen. The most important, the love affair with Essence is real, is present, abiding in our hearts, and it will not change.

There may be dry periods, while one is traveling deeper, when the singing of the heart seems to have abandoned us. To live in devotion to Essence, whether its presence is felt or not, is true devotion. Such fidelity brings one ever deeper within. Blessed is the establishment of knowing we are one with the wave. Subsequently, should we temporarily lose awareness of this love, we can bring our attention back to *being* one with the wave where love's presence is known and felt. Even if the worst possible should happen and everything was ripped away, how could anyone forget this love? What remains is still our love affair with Essence. The only thing we don't have is any way to possibly fully express our gratitude for the abundance we have been given. We can only live moment–to–moment in devotion to this love.

I surrender to the Mystery
In the lap of God, I rest my case
The force that bore this world can carry me
Who am I to question grace?

Who dreamed me into form?
Whose will sustains me?
Who brings what comes my way?
And when I die, who claims me?

from "Pulling in the Oars" by Kirtana

Bibliography

Byron Katie, *Loving What Is* (Harmony Books: New York, 2002).

John de Ruiter, *Unveiling Reality* (Oasis Edmonton Publishing: Edmonton, Canada, 1999).

Gangaji, *You Are That*, Volumes I & II, *Freedom and Resolve: The Living Edge of Surrender* (The Gangaji Foundation: Novato, CA, 1995).

Contacts

John de Ruiter
Oasis
Box 78029 RPO Callingwood
Edmonton, Alberta, Canada T5T6A1
truth@johnderuiter.com
www.johnderuiter.com

Gangaji
The Gangaji Foundation
2245 Ashland Street
Ashland, Oregon 97520
info@gangaji.org
www.gangaji.org

Byron Katie
Byron Katie International
P.O. Box 2110
Manhattan Beach, CA 90267
info@thework.org
www.thework.org

Kirtana
Wild Dove Music
PO Box 1221
Felton, CA 95018
info@kirtana.com
www.kirtana.com

Lyn Mayo
PO Box 787
Woodstock, NY 12498
info@lynmayo.com
www.lynmayo.com

SYDA Foundation
P.O. Box 600
South Fallsburg, NY 12779-0600
www.siddhayoga.org

Acknowledgments

In deep gratitude:

to and Shanti Einolander and Alissa Lukara
for the editing of this book.

to Rodger Stevens, Fred Mayo and Gary Klieiver
for their invaluable contributions.

to loyal friends who provided support and encouragement,
Elaine Fielder, Nicholas La Mattina, Cori Bishop, Jonah Blue,
Lucy Barth, Shoshana Love.

to all others generous folks who kindly read the manuscript
and gave their thoughtful reactions.

to Kirtana whose music has nourished me
through out the writing of this book and for the priceless gift
of agreeing upon the inclusions of her lyrics.

to Paul Clemens and the folks at Blue Dolphin Publishing for
the care with which they have brought this book to readers.

About the Author

Lyn Mayo, Ed.D., has an affinity for small college towns. She grew-up in Ithaca, New York, received her doctorate from the University of Massachusetts in Amherst and lived for twenty-five years in New Paltz. While residing in the Hudson Valley, she was a faculty member for ten years at SUNY New Paltz and then went into full time private practice of psychotherapy. During the writing of this book Lyn lived in the beautiful community of Ashland, Oregon. Currently, she is living again in the Hudson Valley of New York.

The Science of the Soul
On Consciousness and
the Structure of Reality
Geoffrey D. Falk
ISBN: 1-57733-131-1, 340 pp., 6x9, paper, $19.95

Metaphysical Techniques That Really Work
Audrey Craft Davis
ISBN: 1-57733-128-1, 148 pp.,
5.5 x 8.5, paper, $14.95

The System for Soul Memory
Using the Energy System of
Your Body to Change Your Life
Susan Kerr
ISBN: 1-57733-089-7,
256 pp., 5.5 x 8.5, paper,
$14.95

Beyond Death
Confronting the Ultimate Mystery
Christopher Scott
ISBN: 1-57733-077-3, 244 pp., 6x9, paper, $16.95

When Spirits Come Calling
The Open-Minded Skeptic's Guide to After-Death Contacts
Sylvia Hart Wright
Paperback, ISBN: 1-57733-095-1, 256 pp., 6x9,
$15.95; Hardcover, ISBN: 1-57733-125-7, $24.95

O Sane and Sacred Death
First Person Accounts of Death as received in hypnotic regressions
Louise Ireland-Frey, M.D.
ISBN: 1-57733-090-0, 272 pp., 5.5 x 8.5,
paper, $15.95

The Inner Palace
Mirrors of Psychospirituality in Divine and Sacred Wisdom-Traditions
Mitchell D. Ginsberg, Ph.D.
2 Vol. set: paperback, $59.95, ISBN: 1-57733-136-2. Vol. 1, ISBN: 1-57733-103-6, 404 pp.;
Vol. 2, ISBN: 1-57733-111-7, 474 pp.
hardcover, $99.95, ISBN: 1-57733-137-0:
Vol. 1, ISBN: 1-57733-123-0, 404 pp.;
Vol. 2, ISBN: 1-57733-124-9, 474 pp.

Turning to the Source
An Eastern View of Western Mind:
Using Insight Meditation and Psychotherapy for Personal Growth, Health and Wholeness
Dhiravamsa
ISBN: 0-931892-20-1, 256 pp., 6.25 x 9.25, cloth,
$19.95

BOOKS FROM BLUE DOLPHIN PUBLISHING

Awakening Love
The Universal Mission: Spiritual Healing in Psychology and Medicine
Nicholas C. Demetry, M.D. & Edwin L. Clonts, M.D.
ISBN: 1-57733-075-7, 240 pp., 6x9, paper, $14.95

The Art of Letting Go
A Pathway to Inner Freedom
Vidya Frazier, L.C.S.W.
ISBN: 1-57733-112-5, 260 pp., 6 x 9, paper, $16.95

Edgework
Exploring the Psychology of Disease: A Manual for Healing Beyond Diet & Fitness
Ronald L. Peters, M.D., M.P.H.
ISBN: 1-57733-116-8, 284 pp., 6 x 9, paper, $17.95

The One-Minute Healing Experience
Ellen Laura
ISBN: 1-57733-012-9, 120 pp., 5.5 x 8.5, paper, $11.00

The Little Book of Big Feared Truths
Overcoming the Main Obstacle to Healthy Self-Esteem
Herbert S. Demmin, Ph.D.
ISBN: 1-57733-101-X, 128 pp., 5x8, paper, $12.95

Points
The Most Practical Program Ever to Improve Your Self-Image
David A. Gustafson
ISBN: 0-931892-74-0, 192 pp., 5.5 x 8.5, paper, $12.95

Johnson's Emotional First Aid
How to Increase Your Happiness, Peace, and Joy
Victoria Ann Johnson, M.A.
ISBN: 1-57733-015-3, 72 pp., full-color, 7.75 x 10, paper, $15.95

Love, Hope & Recovery
Healing the Pain of Addiction
Joann Breeden
ISBN: 0-931892-77-5, 272 pp., 5.5 x 8.5, paper, $12.95

Printed in the United States
31856LVS00001B/523

9 781577 331513